A SERMON WORKBOOK

A SERMON WORKBOOK

Exercises in the Art and Craft of Preaching

Thomas H. Troeger & Leonora Tubbs Tisdale

 Abingdon Press™

Nashville

A SERMON WORKBOOK:
EXERCISES IN THE ART AND CRAFT OF PREACHING

ISBN 978-1-4267-5778-5

13 14 15 16 17 18 19 20 21 22—10 9 8 7 6 5 4 3 2 1

MANUFACTURED IN THE UNITED STATES OF AMERICA

*We dedicate this book to the students of
Yale Divinity School,
whose intelligence, creativity, passion, and faithfulness in preaching
are an inspiration to us.*

CONTENTS

ACKNOWLEDGMENTS

Books are often many years in the gestation process, and this one comes to birth in the fullness of time—as we complete seven years of co-teaching the introductory preaching class at Yale Divinity School. To say that our preaching colleagueship has been a joy would be an understatement. We have reveled in it, grown from it, been inspired by it, had fun with it, and, in the process, developed a way of teaching preaching that is different from how either of us did it previously. So our first debt of gratitude is to one another. What a gift it is to have a colleague who is a genuine complement intellectually, a partner in faith and prayer, and a fun human being to boot!

The second partner in this process has been the amazing group of students we have taught through the years at Yale Divinity School. They have challenged and affirmed us, inspired and moved us, and consistently embraced the task of preaching with energy, imagination, faithfulness, compassion, and intellect. It is to them we have dedicated this book, for they give us hope for the church and the world! They have also made this book much stronger than it would have been because many have allowed us to use their written exercises to illustrate the principles we discuss. Fifty exercises by former or current students are included in Part II of the workbook, but we could have used many times that number, had space allowed. We count ourselves privileged to teach and to learn from them.

A third group of partners are the adjunct instructors who over the years have led many of the small groups in which students deliver and respond to one another's sermons. Most of them are pastors and chaplains with their own busy ministries, including the regular preparation and delivery of sermons. They have drawn effectively on their years of accumulated homiletical wisdom, and we have learned much from them. They include Bonita Grubbs, Julia Kelsey, Andy Nagy-Benson, Ian Oliver, Susan Olson, Vernice "Hopie" Randall, Eric Smith, Shelly Stackhouse, and an expert in speech coaching, Adrienne Milics.

We also owe a huge debt of gratitude to the former deans of Yale Divinity School, Harry Attridge and Emilie Townes, who have always encouraged our endeavors, who have granted us generous leaves to undertake our research and writing, and who have supported us in our team approach to teaching. We are well aware that it is a luxury these days to have a preaching department with two full-time faculty members and to be in an institution that does not penalize its faculty for team teaching. We are grateful to Yale for affording us the chance to do what we do—and to do it together. And we are also grateful to our research assistant Luanne Panarotti, who has ably and efficiently attended to many of the editorial chores associated with this work and helped keep us sane by keeping the chaos monster at bay!

Finally, we thank our respective spouses, Alfred Tisdale and Merle Marie Troeger, for being our encouragers, our friends, and the best life partners imaginable. You grace our lives more than we can say!

Nora Tubbs Tisdale and Thomas H. Troeger
Yale Divinity School, New Haven, CT
Epiphany 2013

INTRODUCTION: THE WHYS AND HOWS OF THIS WORKBOOK

Welcome to this workbook for learning preaching! Whether you are someone who has never preached before or an experienced local church pastor, whether you are training to become a lay preacher or are engaged in homiletical studies in a theological seminary, this workbook is for you. Its exercises are designed to help you think like a preacher, write like a preacher, and proclaim the good news with imagination, theological integrity, deepened biblical insight, and heartfelt passion.

What's more, these exercises are designed to help you claim or reclaim joy in the sermon preparation process. Over the years that we have co-taught preaching at Yale Divinity School, students have come into our classrooms at all stages of readiness to preach. While some have been excited about the task, others have approached it with fear and trepidation, and still others have viewed it as a necessary but cumbersome chore to be undertaken amid the myriad tasks of ministry. What they have almost universally discovered through their engagement in these exercises is that while preaching does indeed require hard work and dedicated commitment, it can also be fun. Preaching allows us to think creatively and imaginatively, to engage parts of our brain that can go underdeveloped in a purely academic environment, and to give voice to the deepest theological convictions we hold in our hearts and souls. The act of faithful proclamation not only gives hope to its hearers; it also gives joy to those who find themselves better equipped to proclaim the gospel with intelligence, imagination, and love.

Why This Workbook?

We have intentionally designed a workbook of discrete preaching exercises, rather than a comprehensive homiletical textbook with one sustained argument, for a variety of reasons:

1. The electronic age in which we live has fostered an increased aptitude for multitasking. The result is that most of us do not think or operate in our daily lives along textbook lines. Rather, we tend to think in terms of the many discrete tasks we need to address, which represents a different way of organizing human consciousness.

2. We live in an era when we are more aware than ever of the impact diversity has upon our faith and our lives. We need an approach to homiletics that honors the diverse perspectives of different traditions, racial-ethnic groups, and genders, while also allowing the preacher to discover and develop her or his own unique voice and style for proclamation.

3. Many people in this media age are used to brief communications. Consequently, one of the ways to learn to communicate is to start out with shorter exercises. We can work from the exercises to build the capacity for preparing full-length sermons. But the exercises themselves can also serve as brief sermons to be used on occasions when a longer sermon

is not desired—thus communicating with a generation that has become accustomed to listening to "sound bites."

4. Because people enter the study of preaching at many different stages of development, what one person needs the other may have already mastered, and vice versa. We need a flexible workbook so that each person can start at his or her own point of readiness.

5. In the midst of diversity and variation, we need more than ever theological clarity about why we preach and what matters most for human life. We need an approach that has flexibility and variety, while simultaneously helping people give witness to the core of the gospel.

Pedagogical Benefits of the Workbook Model

In addition to all of the personal and cultural benefits a workbook approach to preaching offers, we also believe there are significant pedagogical benefits to be gained from it. Indeed, one of the major reasons we have moved away from a more "lecture-centered" approach to teaching preaching and toward a more "exercise-centered" approach is because it better honors adult learners and the ways they come to new understanding. As Thomas Armstrong has observed,

> For most Americans, the word "classroom" conjures up an image of students sitting in neat rows of desks facing the front of the room, where a teacher either sits at a large desk correcting papers or stands near a blackboard lecturing to students. This is certainly one way to organize a classroom, but it is by no means the only way or the best way. The theory of multiple intelligences suggests that the classroom environment—or classroom *ecology*, if you will—may need to be fundamentally restructured to accommodate the needs of different kinds of learners.[1]

This book represents our effort to offer a "fundamentally restructured" approach to teaching homiletics that honors the many different ways we learn.

While drawing on conventional homiletical works for some of the theory provided in this workbook, we present that theory in a new way. Instead of long chapters, we introduce a homiletical principle and then ask you, the reader, to engage in an exercise that employs the principle. After completion of the exercise, we invite you to reflect—either individually or in small groups—upon what you have learned from the theory and from putting it into practice. You will be integrating theory and practice, a process that is crucial to excellent preaching, and as you reflect upon your experience, you will be developing your skills as a practical theologian.

Our approach also incorporates the best of contemporary learning theory: using, for example, multiple intelligences and sociocultural analysis that foster greater awareness of the diverse contexts in which we preach.

The Importance of Two Voices

We have written this volume in the way that we also teach the introductory preaching course at Yale Divinity School: in two voices, one female and one male, that complement and support one another. In an era when women are still denied access to the pulpit in a number of denominational traditions, we think it critical to have homiletical modeling that posits women and men as partners in the teaching of preaching. Furthermore, we find that our teaching is greatly enriched by both the knowledge and the skills each of us uniquely brings to the task, and by the new ideas that have been sparked by our collaboration in the classroom and in the writing of this book.

After writing about homiletics and teaching preaching in many different schools, churches, and denominational settings, we find that together we are now teaching more creatively than we ever did before. We are also enjoying it more! We invite you to join in the fun.

The Structure of This Workbook

The exercises in this workbook are divided into two parts. In Part I, you will become acquainted with a series of homiletical principles and practices that are essential for good preaching, the theology and theory underlying them, and exercises for engaging them. These exercises are designed to help you to think like a preacher.

The exercises in Part II are designed to help you write like a preacher. Unlike academic writing, crafting sermons requires that you write for the ear rather than the eye and that you attend to the cadences and rhythms of oral speech. Sermon writing also requires the use of vivid imagery and engaging narrative, as well as the integration of head and heart that is often more evident in good literary writing or poetry than in academic prose. The exercises in this section will help you become more proficient in the style of writing that makes for good preaching.

How to Use This Workbook

This workbook is designed so that it can either form the structure for an entire basic course in preaching or be used as a supplemental preaching resource for individual enrichment, informal group study, lay preaching seminars, or use in conjunction with other preaching texts in a seminary course.

1) Structuring an entire course using this workbook

Our own introductory course in preaching includes the following elements, each of which we will discuss briefly:

a. Plenary class sessions

Part I of this workbook, "Thinking Like a Preacher," is highly suitable for classroom use. Each of the fifteen chapters forms a discrete unit that can be used to plan a single class session. The chapters include the following elements: homiletical theology and theory focused on one fundamental practice for preaching, an exercise that immediately engages students in that practice, and questions for group reflection and discussion. When we teach the course, we almost always allow time for discussing the exercises in small groups of three to four. We find that small group work provides everyone, including those who are reticent to speak in a larger group, with an opportunity to share their reflections with others. We then allow the final minutes for whole-class debriefing and wrap-up.

In our course syllabus, we provide students with a list of the topics we will cover during the course, but we don't indicate when they will be covered. Rather, we leave the ordering to our discretion, based on class interests and needs. Every year, we have either added new topics and exercises, or omitted some. We have also left open the possibility of integrating what is happening in our preaching class with other events on campus. For example, during a semester when a photographic exhibit on the Iraq War was displayed in the hallway outside our classroom, we asked students to choose one of the photographs and write a sermon introduction based on it. We then spent the class session discussing the challenges of preaching on a social issue like war.

While the exercises in this workbook provide the core of what we teach in our course—that is, the real "course textbook"—we also have students read four additional homiletical texts in the course of the semester so that they are exposed to a diversity of voices and perspectives on preaching. We devote our entire penultimate class session to answering any questions students might have about matters we have not had the opportunity to address during the course. Students write out their questions on little slips of paper, and we collect them in our sermon "genie jar" and then take turns drawing out questions and answering them aloud.

b. Writing exercises

Part II of this workbook, "Writing Like a Preacher," includes an introductory chapter on writing in the oral/aural style (chapter 16) and thirteen writing exercises (chapter 17–chapter 29) in which students engage the oral/aural style in order to write a one-page "mini sermon" on an assigned topic. The exercises are designed to help students break out of academic modes of writing and to engage their theological imaginations in writing that appeals to the senses and the emotions, as well as to the head and will. They are also designed to help students become more focused and succinct in their sermon writing.

In our own introductory course, students begin having written assignments the second week of class. Thereafter, they turn in one written assignment every week. One of our tasks as instructors is to read all the written assignments immediately after they are turned in to us and to jointly select the best four or five student papers. We then begin the following class session (and all subsequent class sessions) by reading aloud anonymously the best student papers turned in the previous week.

We have discovered several significant benefits from taking this approach. First, students learn a great deal about how to improve their own writing by hearing the best practices of their classmates. Their peers become their teachers, modeling the principles discussed in each chapter. Second, students are (anonymously) rewarded for good homiletical writing and are encouraged to keep at it. Finally, students often find themselves moved, inspired, and even awed by hearing the sermons of their peers. You will see why when you read the model student exercises that have been included in every chapter of Part II!

Class also feels more like worship when we begin it this way. Indeed, for our very last class session, we take the best student papers written in response to the exercise in chapter 29, in which students are asked to preach a sermon to their peers about the purposes of preaching, and design a closing worship service around them.

c. Preaching sections

The third component to our course is preaching sections. Students are divided into preaching sections (no more than ten in each) with either an instructor or a local pastor as section leader. Throughout the course of a semester, each student preaches and receives group critique on two full sermons. Students are videotaped as they preach, and they write brief reflection papers on what they learned from watching themselves on tape. A speech coach meets with them to work on delivery issues.

d. Bringing it all together

In a final course paper, students have an opportunity to integrate what they have learned through the class presentations and discussions, their reading of the four assigned homiletical texts, preaching and listening to their peers preach in their small groups, and engaging in the weekly written exercises. We are often amazed by the learning and growth that has taken place in one short semester!

2) Using this workbook in lay pastor training or as a supplemental seminary course text

One of the audiences we had in mind as we prepared this workbook is people who are preparing to become lay pastors and their instructors. The simplicity of the design and the open-ended nature of the workbook allow instructors to pick and choose the chapters in Part I and the writing exercises in Part II most needed by their particular groups, and to structure a course of any length around them. Because the book virtually teaches itself, a lot of additional preparation on the part of the instructor is not necessarily required. Class sessions could be devoted to engaging in and discussing the exercises, and to continued reflection on the homiletical theology and theory set forth in the various chapters. When the official course is over, individual participants may well want to extend their learning by working through more of the exercises on their own.

This workbook can also easily be used as a supplemental course text in seminary preaching classes. Instructors can simply pick and choose the exercises they want their students to engage and incorporate them into their own course syllabi.

3) Using this workbook informally in an individual or group setting

If you are an individual or group who has decided to use this workbook for your own enrichment, you have at least two options for how to do so. The first option is to work through it methodically, tackling one chapter from Part I and one writing exercise from Part II in each session. We have ordered the topics in Part I of the book in the sequence in which we often teach them, so they flow in a logical and progressive pattern. The important thing to remember is that the writing exercises in Part II of the book are not meant to be engaged *after* completing Part I; they are meant to be undertaken *while* you are working through Part I.

A second option is to begin at a place that would be most helpful to you—perhaps at a place where you are running into difficulties in your own preaching—and to move around within the workbook as you see fit. It is essential, however, that you undertake exercises from both Parts I and II in order to reap the workbook's full benefits.

One of the advantages of group work is that you have a ready-made community of peers with whom to share and reflect on your exercises. While face-to-face engagement is ideal, we can also imagine these conversations happening online if a group of pastors or lay pastors covenanted to work through the exercises together over a period of time.

If you are working individually, it would be good if you could find a preaching partner who would be willing to listen to your exercises and reflect on them with you. Ideally, this person might even commit to work through the exercises with you!

Notes

1. Thomas Armstrong, *Multiple Intelligences in the Classroom*, 2nd ed. (Alexandria, VA: Association for Supervision and Curriculum Development, 2000), 67.

part one

THINKING LIKE A PREACHER

HALLMARKS OF GOOD PREACHING

We assume that many of you already know a considerable amount about preaching. It may be intuitive knowledge, things you have sensed and felt but not yet named to yourself. Through the years you have heard sermons—good, bad, and mediocre—whether in local churches or synagogues, on street corners, via television, in movies, or on the Internet. Even if you are fairly new to a faith tradition, our guess is that you have heard enough sermons to begin forming opinions about what makes them effective or not.

We have designed the exercise in this chapter to tease out some of what you already know and think about preaching. Through it, you will begin to identify some of the hallmarks of good preaching, as well as some of the things that contribute to poor or ineffectual proclamation.

Our goals are threefold: understanding the essential nature of preaching, developing criteria for evaluating sermons, and reassuring novice preachers that they have knowledge about the art and craft of sermons that can help them in their own efforts to proclaim the word of God.

First, when we talk about what makes a sermon "good" or "bad," we begin to understand the essence of preaching itself. For example, if we call a sermon "good" because it stays close to the biblical texts that are read aloud in worship, our judgment reveals that we believe preaching is supposed to be rooted in the word of God as revealed in the Scriptures. The faithful use of the Bible is a part of the essence of preaching. Or, alternatively, if we define "bad" preaching as preaching in which the preacher talks about only himself or herself, rather than focusing on the congregation and its needs and concerns, then we see that another essential hallmark of preaching is attentiveness to the listeners. The exercise in this chapter provides a way for you to carry on the process of these last few sentences about "good" and "bad" sermons, to name your own assumptions about what preaching should be and do.

Second, engaging in this exercise—especially in a group—allows for the development of criteria that can be used in the critique and evaluation of the sermons preached by ourselves, our peers, and our colleagues. When we teach our introductory homiletics course at Yale, we use this exercise to compile a list of attributes that students can then use throughout the term as they critique one another's sermons. Rather than our arbitrarily providing a list of things we are looking for, this process allows the students themselves to provide a list of criteria for evaluating the sermons they preach and hear.

Finally, engaging in this exercise reminds even the most inexperienced of preachers that they actually know far more about preaching than they might have initially thought. None of us approaches the task of learning to preach as a blank slate. Rather, we come to this endeavor with some very helpful knowledge that we have gleaned from our own experiences of preaching—knowledge that can be invaluable to us as we undertake this important task.

EXERCISE: HALLMARKS OF PREACHING

1. Think of one of the most positive experiences of preaching that you have had. It might be a sermon that you have heard, or a preacher whose sermons you have experienced. In a sentence or two, reflect on why that experience of preaching, either the sermon or the preacher, was so positive for you. What was it that made it so? Try to be as specific as possible in naming the particular attributes or principles at work that made it so.

_____

_____

_____

2. Think of one of the most negative experiences of preaching that you have had. It might be a sermon that you have heard, or a preacher whose sermons you have experienced. In a sentence or two, reflect on why that experience of preaching, either the sermon or the preacher, was so negative for you. Specifically, what was it that made it so?

_____

_____

_____

3. Complete the following sentences:

I believe preaching is most effective when . . .

_____

I believe preaching is least effective when . . .

_____

Individual and Small Group Reflection and Discussion

After working individually on these questions, we recommend that participants, if in a group or class setting, break into small groups of three or four and share their answers to the exercise questions with one another. Individuals, groups, or the class as a whole might then reflect on the following questions:

1. What key principles about preaching have emerged from your engagement in this exercise? Try to state the principle as succinctly and clearly as possible, and relate it to the experience you have named.

_____

_____

2. Based on your engagement in this exercise, what are some of the most significant criteria you would posit for use in critiquing your sermons and the sermons of others?

_____

_____

Follow Up (for use in a class or group setting)

Our practice is to have all students hand in this exercise at the end of the class period in which they undertake it. Before the next class session, we read through all the exercises and compile a list of the most frequently cited positive and negative attributes of preaching that emerge from the exercise, grouping them into appropriate categories. We then give students a copy of the listing and encourage them to bring the list with them to preaching sections (where students actually preach their sermons) so that they can use them as criteria for the sermon critique process.

Below is a sample listing, compiled from one of our introductory classes at Yale Divinity School. Please note that we have also indicated places where students can turn in John S. McClure's book *Preaching Words: 144 Key Terms in Homiletics,*[1] one of our course texts, to read further about the concepts and hallmarks identified through this exercise.

STUDENT RESPONSES TO HALLMARKS OF PREACHING EXERCISE

1. Multiple Purposes of Preaching

Moves the listener to a response—change in thoughts, behavior, lifestyle

Encouraging (literally, bestowing courage) by challenging us to need and know Jesus in an immediate, powerful way

Seeks to reframe ideas/stories/beliefs and re-invites its hearers to interact in the world

Presents the ugliness of the cross and the beauty of the empty tomb

Illuminates the Word

Draws you into the Scripture, challenges your assumptions, gives you new eyes, convicts, delivers grace

Preaches "the Truth" (even if I disagree with it)

Appeals to both intellect and emotion

Personal experience and God's Word meet

Focus is on the gospel and the community

Ties together all the threads of the day's liturgy

Engages head, heart, and spirit

Balances head and heart, displaying an intelligence on multiple levels of spiritual leadership

Is challenging, should make you think, transforming

Relevant, courageous, and unusual

Surprising

Confounding

If you want to pursue the purposes of preaching, you can turn to McClure, pp. 118–19, and read: "The New Testament provides several words for preaching, each of which expresses a different purpose . . ."

2. Form or Design of Sermons

Is concise and clear

Presents one idea

Intellectually stimulating, integrative, exciting, positive, hopeful

Use of concrete imagery—creative imagination, vivid examples from real life

Step-by-step unfolding of the image

A clearly articulated focus to the sermon

Accessibility in thought and delivery

Not too long or too short

Some kind of story, narrative, anecdote is told

Uses metaphors and challenges one's idea of God and life

Involves both the head and the heart

If you want to pursue this, McClure gives you a good start with his entries on "form" on pp. 38–39 and "structure" on p. 129.

3. The Person of the Preacher and the Preacher's Delivery

The preacher believes in what she's preaching.

The preacher's own experience and God's Word meet.

The preacher speaks from his/her own experiences and causes you to reflect on your life in a new and challenging way.

Passionate and educated about his or her message

Authenticity/transparency in expressing their desires, doubts, and conviction.

Comfortable and conversational in the pulpit

Open to God, vulnerable with their congregations

Preach like their lives depend on it

Calm and clear, but full of energy

Makes eye contact

Integrity of the preacher is of utmost importance

Exudes calm grace

Makes himself/herself an offering to God

Delivered with active engagement

Studying McClure's list of terms in the Contents, you will discover several terms that expand upon your insights: "authenticity" (pp. 5–6), "delivery" (p. 20), "self-disclosure" (p. 122), and "voice" (pp. 144–45).

4. Role of the Congregation

Reveals knowledge of and relationship with the congregation

Makes a personal connection with the listener

Proclaims the Word while addressing needs particular to the community that is hearing it

Addresses the congregation's corporate situation

Those who listen are in turn prepared to preach.

Those who listen are provoked to thought and action.

A preaching event occurs as a collaboration between speaker and congregation.

Listeners are invited to wrestle with concepts, but are given an invitation to act.

Listeners are allowed to interpret.

Sermons create a unified emotional experience for the community.

Intimate

Meets the congregation's need

If you want to pursue these issues, you can look up "congregational study" on pp. 16–17 of McClure, and when you get to the end of that term, you will find another, related term, "contextual preaching."

5. The Place and Use of the Bible and Theology in Preaching

Employs Scripture and experience to lovingly bring people out of their comfort zones and address real issues of justice to effect change

Balance between tradition, texts, and present reality

It couples the love of Christ with the truth of our brokenness and illustrates how God ultimately goes after us.

Preaching must be grounded in both the biblical text and contemporary life.

A close reading of the Bible passage that invites discussion about how it relates to our lives

Scripture guides the sermon.

McClure helps us find resources for these concerns through his entries on "biblical preaching" (p. 10) and "hermeneutics" (p. 47).

6. The Holy Spirit and Preaching

The preacher is prepared, but also leaves room for the Holy Spirit to move.

One prays, prepares oneself, and presents self as an offering to God (decreasing self so that God can increase).

The Holy Spirit is dwelling in the preaching, bringing everyone into community.

Notes

1. John S. McClure, *Preaching Words: 144 Key Terms in Homiletics* (Louisville, KY: Westminster John Knox Press, 2007).

DIVERSITY IN PREACHING

One of the things we have observed through our years of teaching homiletics is that student expectations vary widely regarding how preaching should look and sound. For example, should the preacher offer sermons from the pulpit while using a manuscript, or preach from the center aisle without notes? Should a sermon last no more than ten minutes, or is the preacher only getting warmed up twenty-five to thirty minutes into the message? Is the preacher expected to focus the sermon on the lectionary Gospel or Epistle reading for the day, to preach regularly as well from the Hebrew scriptures, or to create his or her own lectionary for preaching? Is the preacher expected to show a great deal of emotion in the pulpit or to be more reserved in the expression of feeling?

We believe that it is critically important that these differences in expectations regarding preaching be identified and named early in the learning-to-preach process for a variety of reasons:

First, one of the great gifts a preaching class can offer its students is the opportunity to become more deeply acquainted with the diversity of ways in which effective preaching takes place across denominations, cultures, and traditions. There is no "one right way" to preach. Indeed, there are a myriad of effective preaching styles, and for you, the reader, to become acquainted with some of them not only broadens your own understanding of what preaching can be and do; it also opens you to new possibilities for your own preaching.

Second, when preachers present their sermons to others in a class or group setting, they are not speaking out of a vacuum. Rather, they are coming to proclamation with a whole set of assumptions and expectations regarding what a sermon should be and do—expectations that significantly influence how they proclaim the Gospel. Naming those expectations enables us to hear the preaching of our peers more empathetically and also with greater understanding of the contexts for which their sermons have been prepared.

Third, many pastors will be invited over the course of their careers to preach in a variety of settings other than their own denominations, such as for interfaith or ecumenical worship services, within the worship spaces of other traditions, or in environments other than the sanctuary. Opening ourselves to the practices of others also assists us in becoming more flexible and "ambidextrous" in our own approach to preaching.

Finally, we live in a world where there is a great deal of misunderstanding and miscommunication among and between faith traditions of various kinds. The more we open ourselves to one another and to the new learning we can gain by respecting preaching differences, the more we also break down the dividing walls of hostility that have all too often pitted us against one another in contentious and destructive ways. In dealing with homiletical diversity, we gain insight into the larger theological issue of engaging diversity in the world that God has created. This is hard but important work to do because, as Eleazar S. Fernandez has pointed out, there is a tendency in our society to cover over diversity:

> When confronted with diversity, it is a common pulpit discourse in the United States to project a universal (e.g., equality in the sight of God), which is most often a particular dominant perspective masquerading as universal. This kind of discourse is "assimilationist" and "melting pot" in its intent and consequences.

> An Asian Indian way of thinking, on the other hand, provides an approach that is useful for preachers. Diversity is not reduced to a common denominator or to a universal abstraction. . . . God's love is not a monotonous uniformity, but has multiple expressions in response to the plight of a people, and this, for Asian Americans, is shaped by their experience. [1]

Our honoring and learning from our homiletical diversity is, therefore, a way of developing our ability to present in our sermons God's love not as "a monotonous uniformity" but rather in its "multiple expressions."

What follows is an exercise that invites you to tease out your own pre-understandings and expectations of what preaching should be and do, and then to share your results with one another. While some of you will readily be able to name the faith tradition that is primary for you, others of you will have difficulty with this task, having been a part of a number of diverse traditions yourself. Still others of you may have difficulty because you consider yourself to be in transition between traditions, or a seeker who has not yet settled on any one. For purposes of the exercise, we encourage you to choose one tradition or perspective from which to address the questions, even if it may not be the one where you ultimately find yourself. This will help you be more specific and definitive in your answers. Choose the tradition with which you currently feel most at home, the style of preaching that most effectively engages your heart and mind.

EXERCISE: EXPLORE THE DIVERSITY OF OUR PREACHING EXPECTATIONS

Your name _____
Denominational affiliation or preference _____

In light of your experience and the preaching with which you are most familiar, what are the expectations that you bring to the act of listening and watching a preacher deliver a sermon?

Make notes to the following questions that will help you enter into discussion with classmates. (The numbering of the questions is merely for convenience. There is no implied order of importance. Depending upon the tradition, different elements of preaching will be more or less important.)

1. Do you expect the preacher to choose the text[s] for the sermon, or are they provided by a lectionary? Do you primarily expect the sermon to be based on the Old Testament or New Testament, on the Epistle or Gospel, or on all four lessons? Or are all of these equally acceptable as the sources of biblical texts for preaching?

2. How long do you expect a sermon to be?

3. How do you expect a sermon to be structured? As a logical argument? As a narrative? As a poem, using metaphors and appealing to the imagination? As a verse-by-verse exposition of a particular biblical text? As an exploration of a contemporary issue or a theological theme or _____?

4. What are the dominant names and metaphors for God that you expect to hear in a sermon? Father, Mother, Shepherd, Love, Light, Jesus, Christ, Holy Spirit, the Holy Trinity, or _____?

5. Will the preacher have a full manuscript, notes, or no notes? Will the preacher use visuals of any sort: PowerPoint, video clips, props, or _____?

6. How do you expect preachers to use their voices? Is their vocal tone basically conversational, with the inflections of everyday speech but not a large dynamic range? Do you expect there to be considerable variation in the pace and volume of the speaking voice: for example, building or decreasing in volume as the sermon develops?

7. How do you expect preachers to use their bodies? Do they sit or stand? Do they move a great deal, using many gestures? Do they remain basically still? Do they use direct eye contact or avert the eyes? Are they in a pulpit or the chancel or walking among the congregation or _____?

8. To what extent do you expect preachers to express outwardly and freely their emotions? How much self-disclosure is expected of the preacher: none, some, a lot? Do you expect primarily an appeal to the heart or the mind or both?

9. What do you expect a sermon to accomplish? Conversion to belief in Christ? The deepening of a personal relationship to God? A more informed and mature faith? A sense of fellowship in the body of worshipers? Greater justice in society? Empowering the church for its mission or _____?

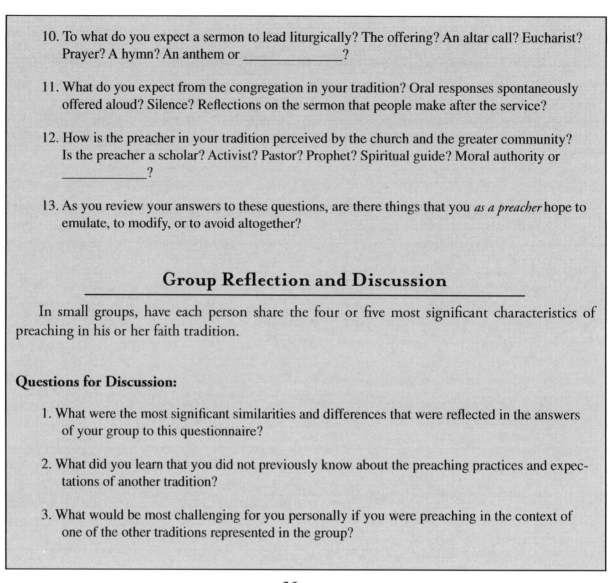

10. To what do you expect a sermon to lead liturgically? The offering? An altar call? Eucharist? Prayer? A hymn? An anthem or _____?

11. What do you expect from the congregation in your tradition? Oral responses spontaneously offered aloud? Silence? Reflections on the sermon that people make after the service?

12. How is the preacher in your tradition perceived by the church and the greater community? Is the preacher a scholar? Activist? Pastor? Prophet? Spiritual guide? Moral authority or _____?

13. As you review your answers to these questions, are there things that you *as a preacher* hope to emulate, to modify, or to avoid altogether?

Group Reflection and Discussion

In small groups, have each person share the four or five most significant characteristics of preaching in his or her faith tradition.

Questions for Discussion:

1. What were the most significant similarities and differences that were reflected in the answers of your group to this questionnaire?

2. What did you learn that you did not previously know about the preaching practices and expectations of another tradition?

3. What would be most challenging for you personally if you were preaching in the context of one of the other traditions represented in the group?

Note

1. Eleazar S. Fernandez, "A Filipino Perspective: 'Unfinished Dream' in the Land of Promise," in *Preaching Justice: Ethnic and Cultural Perspectives,* ed. Christine Marie Smith (Cleveland, OH: United Church Press, 1998), 63–64.

CREATIVE BIBLICAL STUDY FOR PREACHING

In this chapter we will introduce you to a creative Bible study method for sermon preparation that can be used by anyone, whether theologically trained or not. The method is not a substitute for historical-critical exegesis, which we will discuss in the next chapter; it is, however, a creative way to gain a first entry into a text and to view it in a manner that is especially provocative for preaching. The method was developed and introduced by biblical scholar Walter Wink in his book *Transforming Bible Study: A Leader's Guide.*[1] Although we are heavily indebted to Wink, we have revised and adapted his method for the creation of sermons in ways that can be used by either individuals or groups.

In our own teaching, we have used this method effectively in large group classroom settings with the class divided in half and seated in chairs facing one another across a center aisle. The two of us stand on either ends of the room, walking students through the process. We take turns reading the texts and questions to be discussed.

By introducing you to this method of Bible study, we are also introducing you to several significant principles related to preaching, principles that are close in spirit to ways of interpreting the Scriptures that many rabbis have used. Alexander Deeg has written an article exploring how the rabbis blend creative imagination with meticulous attention to the smallest details in a biblical passage.[2] The mixture of imagination and detail often produces striking insights into the life of faith and the character of God, insights that feed good preaching. Deeg observes, "Imagination and meticulousness—they do not fit so easily together. And yet I believe that imagination and meticulousness both belong together, especially when dealing with biblical interpretation and Christian preaching."[3] One of Deeg's most memorable examples is his recounting of a rabbinic interpretation of the story of Jacob's dream in which the patriarch sees a ladder extending from earth to heaven (Genesis 28:10–22). Deeg points out that the rabbis begin not by

asking what the text originally meant or means overall, but *making discoveries in the text.* Because of this, they become aware of little things such as in verse 12, when Jacob sees the ladder and how the angels "ascend and descend." "Ascend and descend"—that is remarkable, say the rabbis. Shouldn't one expect the exact opposite? Shouldn't the angels come "from above," from the heavens, and then come downward to the earth? Does this detail not mean, then, that the angels were along the way with Jacob the whole time? And that the angels are now there during this flight into an unknown land? It would be an assertion not without meaning for moral blemished individuals such as ourselves! Yes, it can mean exactly this, say the rabbis.[4]

19

"Making discoveries in the text" is one of the essential skills that preachers spend a lifetime developing. It is an art that requires close, meticulous reading of the text, and this is often difficult because we assume we already know the text and what it means. We have read it so often or heard it preached so many times that its twists and turns have been worn away in our consciousness. Yet it is those details that can feed our homiletical imaginations and open us to the living Spirit that breathes through the words of Scripture.

Here, for example, is another discovery the rabbis make in the story of Jacob that is rich with sermonic possibilities:

> When the Hebrew text is read closely, then something quite astounding happens as Jacob dreams of the ladder that night. Namely, that evening he took some of the stones in this area and lay on them (Gen 28.11), but in the morning he took "the stone which he set at his head" (v. 18). Between verses eleven and eighteen, over the course of one night in Bethel, only one stone remains from many. "Why is this?" ask the rabbis. And they give a whole range of answers. One of them says:

> "Then the stones began quarreling among themselves. One said, 'Let the righteous one put his head against me,' and the other said, 'Let him put it against me,' until finally the stones coalesced one with the other and became one stone."

> Neither the special night of visions and auditions from Beth-El, nor the special nearness of God in this location can tolerate the stones' argument of who the greatest among them is. A kind of eschatological peace takes place during this night; where God speaks, there the fighting ends—and if it is an argument among stones, then creation will arrive at its peace.[5]

Attending meticulously to one little detail in the biblical text, the shift from "stone" to "stones," stimulates the homiletical imagination with rich possibilities: when earth and heaven are connected, our fragmented creation is made whole. Making such discoveries in the text is the very thing that Walter Wink's method of Bible study encourages.

One of the additional benefits of Wink's method is that it can easily be used with church groups—both as a means for group Bible study and as a way of inviting congregants to participate in the sermon preparation process with us. In recent decades we have come to see that preaching is not something that the preacher does *to* a congregation, but an activity that is done *with* and *on behalf of* a congregation. Preaching arises out of the common life shared in a community of faith and often stays closer to the ground of its hearers if they are actively engaged in the process of sermon preparation. Homileticians Lucy Rose and John McClure have advocated for having a roundtable group Bible study, composed of a diverse group of congregants, become a regular part of the preacher's sermon preparation process.[6] The Wink Bible study method could be used to initiate such a conversation.

Ground Rules for the Bible Study

1. Answer only the question most immediately asked.

2. Do not jump ahead to later verses or other passages in the Bible. Deal with only the passage you have just read or heard.

3. If you have an answer that is completely different from someone else's in the group, share it with the class. However, there is to be no argument about which is the "right" answer.

The leader must be diligent in enforcing these rules. The temptation to race ahead, and to say things like, "but later on in the story it says . . ." will stifle making discoveries in the text that come only from stopping and living with each detail that the questions ask us to consider. We need to model ourselves after the rabbis, patiently living with each word and phrase.

The leader is also responsible for moderating the large group conversation, allowing a sufficient number of diverse voices to be heard, while also keeping the study moving forward so that it can be completed in the time allotted.

EXERCISE: WALTER WINK'S BIBLE STUDY METHOD

Reading the Assigned Text

The individual or group leader first reads aloud Mark 2:1–12 (NRSV version), the story of Jesus healing the paralytic who is let down through the roof by his friends.[7] If the story is read in a group setting, it is good to invite participants to close their eyes so that they can actually envision the scene in their own imaginations as it unfolds.

Reflecting on the Text Verse by Verse

Next, the individual or group leader reads through the passage very slowly, verse by verse (or partial verse by partial verse), inviting time for reflection on the questions that follow each. If this is a group setting, allow time first for individual reflection, and then for large group reflection on the questions.

Engaging the Bible Study {PRIVATE}

Verse 1: When he returned to Capernaum after some days, it was reported that he was at home.
You hear the report that Jesus is back home; write your thoughts about this news.

_____

Verse 2: So many gathered around that there was no longer room for them, not even in front of the door; and he was speaking the word to them.
Where are you in the crowd? Up close, in the middle, on the edge, off at a distance?

_____

What do you see?

_____

What do you hear?

_____

What are you thinking?

_____

Verse 3: Then some people came, bringing to him a paralyzed man, carried by four of them.
For a moment, you are one of those carrying the paralytic. At this point, you have not yet discovered that you cannot get to Jesus.
What has been involved in carrying the paralytic with your friends?

_____

What are you thinking on the journey?

_____

Now switch roles: you are the paralytic.
What has been involved?

What are you thinking on the journey?

Verse 4a: And when they could not bring him to Jesus because of the crowd,
The crowd blocks the way. You are one of the four friends.
Name your initial reactions and strategies that come to mind for handling the situation.

Verse 4b: they removed the roof above him; and after having dug through it,
You are digging the roof apart.
What are you thinking?

Verse 4c: they let down the mat on which the paralytic lay.
What do you think as the opening is completed and you lower your friend?

Switch roles: you are the paralytic.
Initial reactions?

Digging of roof?

Being lowered?

Verse 5a: When Jesus saw their faith,
Whose faith is seen? To whom does "their" refer?

What is the significance of this statement?

Verse 5b: he said to the paralytic, "Son, your sins are forgiven."
You are the friends and you hear the words.
What is your reaction?

Switch roles: you are the paralytic and hear the words.
What is your reaction?

Verses 6 and 7: Now some of the scribes were sitting there, questioning in their hearts, "Why does this fellow speak in this way? It is blasphemy! Who can forgive sins but God alone?"
You are a scribe.
What matters most to you in life?

Chapter 3

For what good reasons are you concerned about what Jesus is doing?

_____

Verses 8 and 9: At once Jesus perceived in his spirit that they were discussing these questions among themselves; and he said to them, "Why do you raise such questions in your hearts? Which is easier, to say to the paralytic, 'Your sins are forgiven,' or to say, 'Stand up and take your mat and walk'?"

You are still a scribe.

What is your reaction to Jesus speaking your thoughts?

_____

What is his answer to your question and why?

_____

Switch roles. You are a friend of the paralytic and you have just heard this entire exchange between Jesus and the scribes.

What are you thinking?

_____

What do you want to say?

_____

Switch roles. You are the paralytic.

What are you thinking?

_____

What do you want to say?

_____

Verses 10 and 11: "But so that you may know that the Son of Man has authority on earth to forgive sins"—he said to the paralytic—"I say to you, stand up, take your mat and go to your home."

You are a scribe.

What do you hear Jesus saying?

_____

You are a friend.

What do you hear Jesus saying?

_____

You are the paralytic.

What do you hear Jesus saying?

_____

What are the reactions to Jesus' words by:

The crowd?

_____

The scribes?

_____

The friends?

_____

The paralytic?

_____

Verse 12: And he stood up, and immediately took the mat and went out before all of them; so that they were all amazed and glorified God, saying, "We have never seen anything like this!"
What are the reactions of the crowd? The scribes? The friends? The paralytic?

Reflection: Concluding Questions for Individual or Group

1. Take a few minutes and identify one potential idea for developing a sermon related to this text. Share the ideas aloud (if in a group).

2. What did you learn from this exercise about preparing a sermon from a biblical text?

For Ongoing Reflection

This biblical text poses many pastoral and theological challenges for the preacher. How do we preach the healing stories of Jesus when there are people within our congregations who have longed for healing and have not received it? What is the difference between "healing" and "cure"? What is the relationship between sin and sickness?

Kathy Black's book *A Healing Homiletic: Preaching and Disability* is an excellent resource for helping us think more deeply about such issues. She comments, "When cure is not currently possible, healing can happen through the supportive accepting community; through our own ability (undergirded by God's strength and the support of others) to make it through the hard times; and through the different, new possibilities that are open for us."[8]

She also devotes an entire section of her chapter entitled "Paralysis" to a study of this passage from Mark 2.[9]

Notes

1. Walter Wink, *Transforming Bible Study: A Leader's Guide* (Nashville: Abingdon Press, 1980).

2. Alexander Deeg, "Imagination and Meticulousness, Haggadah and Halakhah in Judaism and Christian Preaching," *Homiletic* 34:1 (2009), 1-11, accessed July 1, 2013, http://www.homiletic.net/index.php/homiletic/article/view/33151544. We are drawing heavily here on Deeg's work.

3. Ibid., 2.

4. Ibid., 5, emphasis added.

5. Ibid., 5. The distinction between the plural "stones" in Genesis 28:11 and the singular "stone" in 28:18 is kept in the King James Version but not in the New Revised Standard Version. Deeg's rabbinic quotation is from *The Book of Legends/Sefer ha-Aggada: Legends from Talmud and Midrash*, by Chajim Nachman Bialik and Yehoschua Hana Ravnitzky (New York: Schocken, 1992), 45.

6. See Lucy Atkinson Rose, *Sharing the Word: Preaching in the Roundtable Church* (Louisville, KY: Westminster John Knox Press, 1997), and John S. McClure, *The Roundtable Pulpit: Where Leadership and Preaching Meet* (Nashville: Abingdon Press, 1995).

7. We are indebted here not only to Wink's book but also to my (Tom's) experience of Wink leading a Bible study on this very text, using this method as he was first developing it many years ago.

8. From Kathy Black, *A Healing Homiletic: Preaching and Disability* (Nashville: Abingdon Press, 1996), 42.

9. Black, *A Healing Homiletic*, 104–23.

BIBLICAL EXEGESIS FOR PREACHING

There are a number of different ways to read and interpret biblical texts for preaching. One is the Walter Wink-style Bible study method that we described in chapter 3 that has many affinities with rabbinic forms of scriptural interpretation. This method collapses the historical distance between us and the text and invites us to enter into the world of the text, standing in the shoes of its various characters, paying attention to its twists and turns, and thinking imaginatively about them.

A second method, the method of historical-critical exegesis, requires that we distance ourselves from the text so that we ask questions about its historical setting, authorship, the meanings of words in their original language, and its larger canonical context in order to deepen our understanding of its potential meanings. This method serves as a check upon eisegesis (that is, reading into the text what we would like for it to say) and helps us balance the more imaginative approach outlined in the prior chapter with the best tools of critical biblical scholarship. These are not opposite methods, but rather complementary ways of listening for the living word of God. Both methods are a form of what scholars call "hermeneutics." James Earl Massey observes, "Hermeneutical work grants understandings that are basic for dealing with the nature, range, and import of the Scriptures. . . . Simply stated, *hermeneutics* is that science or method by which the meaning in a textual passage is sought, discovered, and then related and applied to one's own cultural context."[1] Responsible preachers use varied forms of hermeneutics because they realize there is "no monolithic interpretation of the biblical text."[2]

Homiletician Fred Craddock once said that there are three chairs the preacher sits in, either literally or figuratively, while preparing a sermon. The first chair is an easy chair in which the preacher prays over the passage, engages it in a first reading, and seeks the Spirit's guidance as she or he goes about the task of sermon preparation. This is an appropriate chair in which to engage in a *lectio divina* reading of the biblical text,[3] pausing over words and phrases to ponder their meaning for contemporary life, or in the kind of Bible study Wink prescribes.

The second chair is the study or desk chair. Here the pastor lays out before her all the commentaries and study aids she has at her disposal, and also visits favorite websites that over time have proven themselves reliable and sound. She undertakes serious scholarly investigation into the text, engaging in conversation with authors who have spent their lives studying the Scriptures.

The final chair is the writing chair—often located in front of a computer. Here the minister begins actually composing the sermon, bringing the insights gained from chairs one and two into focus in a sermon that bridges the distance between "then" and "now."

In this chapter, we are going to engage in an exercise that demonstrates how the tools and methods of historical-critical exegesis might be used effectively in chair number two while preparing a sermon on Philippians 2:1–11. These methods are essential tools for every preacher because "this tendency to identify what Scripture says with what we have been told it says is one of the main obstacles in the way to a liberating interpretation of the Bible."[4] Historical-critical methods help us to place a biblical passage "in its historical setting and ask the question of the direction of God's action in that text. Then, and only then, can we seek to apply the text to our own time."[5]

Most of the resources we have used in undertaking our exegesis of the Philippians text are books that are handily ready on our study shelves. We also limited ourselves to two hours of research so as to simulate the time available for exegetical work in the life of a busy pastor.

At the end of this exercise, we will ask you to identify possible sermon themes that might arise out of historical-critical engagement with the Philippians text, so be thinking about sermon possibilities as we engage in the exegetical process. Some people are under the mistaken impression that they must wait until they get to the end of their exegesis before they start to cogitate about the sermon, but in reality we find seasoned preachers often interweave their scholarly study and their homiletical musings. If ideas start flowing, write them down. Eventually you will have to choose a particular direction for the sermon, but at this point it is more important to leave yourself open to the varied possibilities that your study awakens.

Engaging in Historical-Critical Exegetical Study of a Text for Preaching

Philippians 2:1–11

1) Read the text in multiple translations.

On the following page, you will find Philippians 2:1–11 in three different translations: the New Revised Standard Version (NRSV), the King James Version (KJV), and *The Message*. We have included the NRSV because it was put together by a team of biblical scholars and is representative of the kind of translation that is preferable for scholarly research. We have included the KJV because it is a historic and much beloved translation that is still used as the primary worship Bible in many contexts, and it is the translation members of an older generation often know by heart. Finally, we have included *The Message* because it represents a paraphrased version of the Bible prepared by one interpreter. While it is not preferable for scholarly research, it does open up new possibilities for biblical language and its use in contemporary life.

If you are in a group setting, have the leader of the group read the Philippians passage aloud from the NRSV, while those who are listening follow along in one of the other two translations. As you do so, note the significant differences in how the two translations render the text into English.

If you are using this workbook alone, read through the NRSV version of the text, and then through one or both of the other translations, noting the most significant translation differences.

Philippians 2:1–11 in Three Versions

1-4 If you've gotten anything at all out of following Christ, if his love has made any difference in your life, if being in a community of the Spirit means anything to you, if you have a heart, if you care—then do me a favor: Agree with each other, love each other, be deep-spirited friends. Don't push your way to the front; don't sweet-talk your way to the top. Put yourself aside, and help others get ahead. Don't be obsessed with getting your own advantage. Forget yourselves long enough to lend a helping hand. 5-8 Think of yourselves the way Christ Jesus thought of himself. He had equal status with God but didn't think so much of himself that he had to cling to the advantages of that status no matter what. Not at all. When the time came, he set aside the privileges of deity and took on the status of a slave, became *human*! Having become human, he stayed human. It was an incredibly humbling process. He didn't claim special privileges. Instead, he lived a selfless, obedient life and then died a selfless, obedient death—and the worst kind of death at that—a crucifixion. 9-11 Because of that obedience, God lifted him high and honored him far beyond anyone or anything, ever, so that all created beings in heaven and on earth—even those long ago dead and buried—will bow in worship before this Jesus Christ, and call out in praise that he is the Master of all, to the glorious honor of God the Father. *[The Message]*	1 If there be therefore any consolation in Christ, if any comfort of love, if any fellowship of the Spirit, if any bowels and mercies, 2 Fulfil ye my joy, that ye be likeminded, having the same love, being of one accord, of one mind. 3 Let nothing be done through strife or vainglory; but in lowliness of mind let each esteem other better than themselves. 4 Look not every man on his own things, but every man also on the things of others. 5 Let this mind be in you, which was also in Christ Jesus: 6 Who, being in the form of God, thought it not robbery to be equal with God: 7 But made himself of no reputation, and took upon him the form of a servant, and was made in the likeness of men: 8 And being found in fashion as a man, he humbled himself, and became obedient unto death, even the death of the cross. 9 Wherefore God also hath highly exalted him, and given him a name which is above every name: 10 That at the name of Jesus every knee should bow, of things in heaven, and things in earth, and things under the earth; 11 And that every tongue should confess that Jesus Christ is Lord, to the glory of God the Father. [King James Version]	1 If then there is any encouragement in Christ, any consolation from love, any sharing in the Spirit, any compassion and sympathy, 2 make my joy complete: be of the same mind, having the same love, being in full accord and of one mind. 3 Do nothing from selfish ambition or conceit, but in humility regard others as better than yourselves. 4 Let each of you look not to your own interests, but to the interests of others. 5 Let the same mind be in you that was in Christ Jesus, 6 who, though he was in the form of God, did not regard equality with God as something to be exploited, 7 but emptied himself, taking the form of a slave, being born in human likeness. And being found in human form, 8 he humbled himself and became obedient to the point of death—even death on a cross. 9 Therefore God also highly exalted him and gave him the name that is above every name, 10 so that at the name of Jesus every knee should bend, in heaven and on earth and under the earth, 11 and every tongue should confess that Jesus Christ is Lord, to the glory of God the Father. [New Revised Standard Version]

2) Discuss in small groups (if in a class) or identify on your own your initial responses to the text.

What questions arose in your mind as you heard this text read aloud that you would like to explore further through your own scholarly study of the text?

3) Gather resources of biblical scholarship.

Here are the standard works we drew upon in writing this chapter. There are endless numbers of reference books, but we chose these as reliable resources used by preachers of many traditions:

> *Harper Collins Study Bible*
> *Harpers Bible Dictionary*
> *Harpers One-Volume Bible Commentary*
> *Philippians. Interpretation: A Bible Commentary for Teaching and Preaching*
> *The Women's Bible Commentary*
> *Feasting on the Word, Year B, Vol. 1*

4) Who wrote this letter and when?

The *Harper Collins Study Bible* tells us that Paul wrote this letter to Christians in the city of Philippi, a Roman colony in the province of Macedonia. Paul, along with Timothy, Silas, and others, had visited this city some years before (around 50 CE) during his second missionary journey (see Acts 16:11–40). There he had founded a church whose members Paul regards with special affection. Paul wrote this letter while in prison, though we're not sure where, probably in the mid to late 50s or early 60s CE.[6]

5) What kind of city was Philippi? What characterized its life and culture?

When we are reading Philippians, we are reading someone else's mail. Paul did not send the letter to us but to the members of the church at Philippi. Reading someone else's mail can be baffling because the sender and the receiver often take for granted knowledge about persons, events, locations, and cultural assumptions, of which we are completely ignorant. Statements that make perfect sense to the sender and receiver may perplex us and leave us wondering exactly what lies behind the words we are reading. I, Tom, remember once renting a summer cottage and reading postcards that lay out on an antique desk. The cards had been sent some eighty years earlier from Europe to the United States. Nearly every card said, "I'm so proud of Emma" or "Can't get over the news about Emma." But no card ever said exactly what happened with Emma! The same is sometimes true when we read Paul: we wonder precisely what lies behind his words.

One way to fill in the gaps is to learn about the city or region to where the letter was sent. When, for example, I look up Philippi in a Bible dictionary, I discover that despite "strong Roman influence, the variety of Philippi's religious life suggests that its inhabitants, noncitizens included, were more mixed in their backgrounds. Roman gods such as Jupiter and Mars had their cults, but the Thracian goddess Bendis remained very popular, and sanctuaries to gods from Egypt and to Cybele, a Phrygian goddess, are also known."[7] Such information is rich with homiletical possibilities. Preachers can bring Paul's letter alive by describing the pluralistic, religious culture that characterized the ancient city.

For example, imagine what it must have been like to hear Paul's letter read aloud in a city with a cult dedicated to Jupiter, who in the Roman scheme of things "was sovereign by virtue of his supreme rank, and by the patronage derived from the exercise of the supreme power."[8] Consider how radically different—and possibly baffling—Paul's letter must have sounded when he described a Christ who "though he was in the form of God, did not regard equality with God as something to be exploited, but emptied himself, taking the form of a slave." Residents of ancient Philippi who had been raised on a theology of Jupiter's supreme power might be puzzled by Christ's self-emptying action in the same way that many people in our competitive, power-obsessed world are.

Placing Paul's letter in its historical setting has opened homiletical possibilities that we otherwise would have missed. Scholars generally do not make the leaps between ancient times and contemporary life that are required for creating sermons, but the scholars provide us with the materials we need to think imaginatively about the culture in which the letter was received. It is then up to us preachers to suggest parallels and resonances between Paul's congregation in Philippi and those who listen to us here and now. When we situate the letter in the context of its first readers, the sermon does not emerge straight out of the biblical passage, but rather out of the relationship between the text and the environment in which it was received. Of course, we will never know precisely what went on in the Philippians' heads and hearts, but learning about their pluralistic religious world brings the letter alive and makes clear how Christ's self-emptying love challenged the surrounding theologies of sovereign power.

I supplement my reading about Philippi by going online and looking at pictures of the city, finding several websites that feature photographs of the surrounding land, the ancient ruins, and locations where Paul probably preached. Sometimes while looking at these pictures I read the biblical text aloud, imagining what it must have been like to hear Paul's letter read aloud in its original setting. Even if my reading does not fill in all the gaps in my understanding, it gives me a sense of the reality of Paul's ministry and the community to whom he was reaching out through his letter.

6) What is the church context? What was going on with the Philippians?

It sounds like the Philippians were having trouble getting along. Why? Fred Craddock posits several possible reasons. Perhaps there was polarization within the church around the two women, Euodia and Syntyche, who had worked faithfully with Paul in the past but were now at odds with one another (see 4:2–3). Or perhaps dissension had been generated by those who sought to bring elements of Judaism into the faith and practice of the church (see 3:1b–6). Or perhaps people were divided within the church over the ministry of Paul himself. As Craddock notes, "The relationships of ministers to congregations are very complex and directly affect the relationships of the members to each other."[9] Craddock observes that Paul begins chapter 2 by recalling their life as a community formed in the gospel, using a number of key words he had also used in chapter 1: joy, fellowship, love, partnership, affection, unity, and mind-set or attitude: "Rather than portraying their past as negative and inadequate, a dark backdrop against which to cast appeals for more conversations, Paul lifts to the conscious level those qualities of common life by which the church has been identified and sustained. By rejecting the guilt trip approach, Paul is able to nourish his exhortation with the most unused resource in the church: who the members are and what they already know."[10]

"That which will make Paul's joy complete is concord and harmony in the church at Philippi."[11] "Paul regarded as inappropriate to the body of Christ the selfish eye, the pompous mind, the ear hungry for compliments and the mouth that spoke none, the heart that had little room for others, and the hand that served only the self."[12]

Paul tells the Philippians instead to have the same mind, the same attitude that was in Christ Jesus. And he quotes a hymn that most likely was used in liturgical contexts to remind them of how Christ has acted in relation to them.

7) *What is the literary form of the passage?*

Philippians is a letter, and in the ancient world, letters had certain features. A commentary can help us understand the structure of the letter, and thus provide a larger context for our reading of Philippians 2:1–11.

1:1–2 is a salutation, a greeting that ends with "grace to you and peace from God our Father and the Lord Jesus Christ."

1:3–11 is a thanksgiving. Paul's gratitude for the Philippians is extensive. He obviously loves this congregation, and he deeply appreciates their partnership in the gospel.

1:12–4:20 constitutes the body of the letter. Paul recounts his circumstances as a prisoner and his hope in the gospel. At the end of chapter 1, Paul turns toward the congregation at Philippi and tells them to live their lives in a manner worthy of Christ's gospel. Then he leads into 2:1–11.[13]

One thing to keep in mind when preaching from a letter is that reading these letters aloud was one of the earliest forms of preaching in the Christian church. Consequently, we might invite a congregation to hear this text read aloud during worship as if from one of their former pastors, Paul, who is now in jail.

It is also helpful to remember that adopting a letter form for a sermon is still a legitimate option for preaching today. Think for instance of Martin Luther King Jr.'s "Letter from a Birmingham Jail" or Dietrich Bonhoeffer's "Letters from Prison."

4:21–23 is a closing blessing. It gives the letter a sense of liturgical closure, the same effect as when a preacher sends us out from the service with a benediction, and in this way it reinforces the reading of the letter as an act of proclamation.

8) *Note any shifts in form. Philippians 2:6–11 is a hymn.*

We immediately notice that the layout of the text on the page has changed: "These verses, as their format shows, are widely regarded as a pre-Pauline Christ hymn."[14] From ancient times up until today, hymns are the theology that people are most apt to know by heart: "[H]ymns are the poor person's poetry and the ordinary person's theology."[15] Their concision and imagery and the fact that hymns are nearly always sung, or in ancient times intoned, make them especially memorable. If these verses were in fact a beloved hymn of the church at Philippi, imagine what an effective rhetorical strategy Paul is using. He appeals to what is close to their hearts in order to win them over to living as Christ lived. The command "*Every knee should bend* was probably a liturgical signal for the whole congregation to bow down in recognition of Christ's status as *Lord* (2:11)"[16] Paul, then, is invoking music and worship, two of the most moving practices of the congregation, to persuade them of their need to have "the same mind" that "was in Christ Jesus" (2:5).

Just as hymnologists today often provide a theological and poetic analysis of hymn texts, we can do the same with this biblical text. The Philippians hymn basically tells the Christ story in three movements: pre-existence, earthly career, and glorification.[17] One way to gain a deeper understanding of it is to outline or diagram the trajectory it takes. This text from Philippians might be diagrammed as follows:

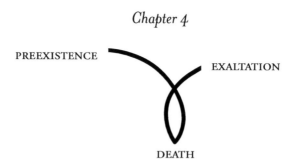

PREEXISTENCE • EXALTATION • DEATH

The hymn moves from Christ's pre-existence before all creation with God (2:6) to his existence on earth (2:7–8) to his post-existence with God in heaven (2:9–11). The hymn also follows the trajectory of the descent of Christ as he empties himself and takes on human form (2:6–8), followed by the upward movement of God's exaltation and glorification of him (2:9–11). Finally, note that there is a change of agent in the middle of this passage. While it is Christ who does all the acting up until verse 9—relinquishing claims, emptying self, becoming human, serving, obeying, dying—it is God who acts thereafter: exalting, celebrating Christ's name, and glorifying.

The very fact that Paul uses a hymn suggests that we might want to build the singing of a hymn into the body of the sermon itself or immediately following the sermon with a hymn based on this passage, thus carrying the message of the sermon home to the hearts of all who sing:

> At the Name of Jesus, every knee shall bow,
> Every tongue confess Him King of glory now;
> 'Tis the Father's pleasure we should call Him Lord,
> Who from the beginning was the mighty Word.
>
> Humbled for a season, to receive a name
> From the lips of sinners unto whom He came,
> Faithfully He bore it, spotless to the last,
> Brought it back victorious when from death He passed.
>
> Bore it up triumphant with its human light,
> Through all ranks of creatures, to the central height,
> To the throne of Godhead, to the Father's breast;
> Filled it with the glory of that perfect rest.
>
> In your hearts enthrone Him; there let him subdue
> all that is not holy, all that is not true.
> Crown him as your captain in temptation's hour;
> let his will enfold you in its light and power.[18]

9) Compare translations, attending to the different words they employ.

Unless we can read the New Testament in Greek, we are dependent upon translations, and no one translation ever captures all the meanings, nuances, and associations of the original. This is why it is important to read the passage in several translations. Different versions will bring out different nuances in the text. Take for example the important phrase "Let the same mind be in you that was in Christ Jesus" (2:5). A cursory reading might suggest that because this is addressed to the whole congregation, not just one individual, Paul is in effect saying, "You ought to agree on everything." For that is the everyday meaning in English of the phrase "having the same mind." But the paraphrase from *The Message* suggests a different understanding of the Greek: "Think of yourselves the way Christ Jesus thought of himself." Fred Craddock specifically rejects our initial reading and points out that "mind" (*phroneo*) does not mean agreeing on everything, but rather having a common attitude or orientation.[19]

We find a similar variety of translations at the start of verse 7, which reads in the NRSV Christ "emptied himself." The KJV renders this with the phrase "made himself of no reputation." *The Message* stresses the theological dimension: "He set aside the privileges of deity." Craddock points out that "emptied himself" (*ekenose*) is virtually synonymous with the word "poor" in 2 Corinthians 8:9 (Christ was rich but became poor).[20] These various understandings of the original Greek open up a range of homiletical possibilities. A preacher might choose to develop a sermon around a single translation or might use all of them to provide multiple perspectives upon the meaning of Christ's coming among us. The important homiletical principle is that comparing translations and studying key words can lead preachers to richer, deeper readings of biblical texts and subsequently to richer, deeper sermons!

10) Consider theological interpretations of the hymn through history.

When preachers are struggling to create a sermon on a particular text, it is easy for them to forget that they are not the first ones to wrestle with the passage. Justo and Catherine González warn against "Lone Ranger" Bible study, in which pastors undertake Bible study either in isolation, or in the company of people who are similar to themselves in terms of class, race, and culture. Consequently, "biblical interpretation fails to be challenged by others, either because they share our own perspective, or because, since they differ from us, we classify them as "Tontos" whose perspectives we need not take into account."[21] González and González challenge us to open ourselves in whatever ways we can to the voices of people of the past and the present who challenge our own interpretive assumptions, and who read the Bible with radically different eyes than our own. One way to do this, especially if we are working alone in our study, is to imagine a text being read in different contexts, such as an underground church in Nazi Germany or a slum in the Dominican Republic.[22]

We also can consider the great cloud of witnesses who have gone before us preachers and who have pondered and cogitated upon the very verses that are challenging us. It is often revealing and homiletically productive to consider how our forebears dealt with the passage.

Theologian Martha Moore-Keish traces some of the history of interpretation of the Philippians hymn in her article in the *Feasting on the Word* commentary: "In the early centuries of Christianity, this text provided an argument against those who questioned Christ's status as equal with God."[23] Athanasius of Alexandria, writing to counter the Arians in the fourth century, used the hymn as evidence that Christ was not just a divinely called human being, but also one who was equal with God from the beginning and who willingly took on the "form of a slave" (2:7).

Writing in the sixteenth century, John Calvin held up Christ's voluntary humbling of self as a model for Christian living. Calling Christians away from prideful living and toward a life of self-denial, this text was used to inspire greater devotion to Christ with promise that those who humble themselves will eventually be exalted by God with Christ.[24]

In the twentieth century, Swiss theologian Karl Barth wove the focus on Christ's humiliation and Christ's exaltation together with Christ's roles as prophet, priest, and king in his doctrine of reconciliation: "As Servant, Christ acts humbly as our priest to redeem us from the sin of pride; as Lord, he exalts humanity by grace to royal partnership with God, liberating us from the sin of self-abasement."[25]

A preacher might take these interpretations and use them in a sermon created around the theme: different meanings of a favorite hymn. We can imagine starting the sermon by asking people to think of a favorite hymn and what it means to them. Was it sung by a parent when they were growing up? Was it sung at some special occasion, a baptism, wedding, funeral? The sermon could then shift to the observation that today's reading from Philippians includes a hymn that has been a favorite down through the ages and has inspired people living in different times and facing different challenges. Next, the preacher might review the history of interpretation. Finally, the sermon could explore what Paul's hymn means now for us. Does it mean what it did in the past? Does it have some new meaning for us? Such a sermon fills one of the major roles of preaching: to develop the historical consciousness of congregations so that their understanding of faith, the church, and Christianity is larger than the limits of their personal experience.

11) Consider the text in the context of the Christian Year.

Paul's hymn about Christ's self-emptying love appears in the lectionary every year on Palm Sunday. If you preach in a church that uses the lectionary, this means that year after year the Philippian hymn helps to frame our understanding of Holy Week: "The hymn stands in the church's Scripture not only to define lordship and discipleship, but also as a judgment upon the kind of triumphalism that abandons the path of service and obedience."[26]

The hymn's placement on the Sunday when most churches re-enact the parade that preceded Christ's passion can awaken a wealth of homiletical possibilities for the preacher. For example, a preacher can move back and forth between the lines of the hymn and the scenes of holy week. The hymn boldly announces Christ "emptied himself, taking the form of a slave." What does that great theological affirmation look like on a human scale that we can understand? Holy Week tells us it looks like a man with a towel bending to wash his disciples' feet, someone who breaks bread and pours wine, someone who prays fervently on the night of his arrest while his best friends sleep.

The hymn proclaims "God also highly exalted him." What does that look like? It looks like an empty tomb and someone standing outside who is mistaken for the gardener. It looks like a stranger who walks at our side and breaks bread with us. It looks like someone cooking fish on the lakeshore. The hymn conveys the grandeur of what Christ has done; the Gospel scenes depict what it cost him and the wonder that followed. The dialogue between the hymn and Holy Week will give the sermon life, a dynamism that arises from the juxtaposition of hymnic, theological language and the graphic human stories in the gospels.

12) To whom should this text be preached?

We are aware that this passage has frequently been used in the past to admonish women and slaves to submit to abusive husbands or masters. It is important to remember, however, that the hymn starts not with the suffering Christ, but with the Christ who is equal to God and who *voluntarily* empties himself. There is no forced servitude here.

Pheme Perkins writes in the *Women's Bible Commentary*, "The poor in Latin America who are told to suffer like Christ rather than struggle for freedom, or abused women whose ministers tell them to submit to husbands, are not in the position to copy the Christ of this hymn. Its challenge is addressed to persons of some status and power, just as Christ had the status of God. In order to preach a gospel that centers on a crucified person and that brings persecution in its wake, such people must empty themselves."[27]

13) Put it all together by narrowing the focus of your sermon.

Our exploration of Philippians 2:1–11 has revealed far more materials and approaches than a preacher could ever use in a single sermon. Beginning preachers sometimes get so excited by the wealth of materials they discover that they "want to get everything in." But "getting everything in" is a recipe for homiletical disaster. The result is a sermon that is a grab bag of assorted insights and asides, but which has no coherent structure for the listener to follow, no central story or image or argument that presents the gospel in a compelling, comprehensible way.

The fact that we have more material than we can use does *not* mean we have wasted precious time. All that extra material has two great values. First of all, it will give us a feeling of confidence that we possess a sound, informed grasp of the passage on which we are preaching. Secondly, this is a passage that comes up every year in the lectionary, so the materials we do not use this time we may use another. Even if our tradition does not follow the lectionary, Philippians 2:1–11 is one of the great texts from the Apostle Paul that nearly all preachers return to again and again. Just because your knowledge of the passage does not find its way into this Sunday's sermon does not mean it will be wasted in the future.

Having affirmed the value of doing thorough research, we are still faced with the question "What will be the focus of my sermon?" To help you get started in answering that question, we invite you to complete the following exercise.

EXERCISE: MOVING FROM BIBLICAL EXEGESIS TO PREACHING FOCUS AND FUNCTION

Write a focus and function statement for a sermon based on Philippians 2:1–11 and the exegetical work that we have done in this chapter.

Thomas Long defines a *focus statement* as "a concise description of the central, controlling and unifying theme of the sermon. In short, this is what the whole sermon will be 'about.'" He defines a *function statement* as "a description of what the preacher hopes the sermon will create or cause to happen for the hearers. Sermons make demands upon the hearers, which is another way of saying that they provoke change in the hearers (even if the change is a deepening of something already present). The function statement names the hoped-for change."[28] Focus and function statements should (a) grow directly out of the exegesis of the biblical text; (b) be clearly related to each other; and (c) be clear, unified, and simply stated.[29]

1. Focus statement (ten words maximum)

_____

2. Function statement (ten words maximum)

_____

Are your statements simple, clear, direct, coherent, and faithful to the word of God that is emerging from the exegesis? Look critically at what you have written, and keep tinkering if you need to, because the clearer you get these statements, the clearer your sermon will be.

Notes

1. James Earl Massey, "Hermeneutics and Pulpit Work," in *Interpreting God's Word for Today: An Inquiry into Hermeneutics from a Biblical Theological Perspective*, ed. Wayne McCown and James Earl Massey (Anderson, IN: Warner Press, Inc., 1982), 250.

2. Teresa L. Fry Brown, "The Action Potential of Preaching," in *Purposes of Preaching*, ed. Jana Childers (St. Louis: Chalice Press, 2004), 52.

3. For a brief introduction to *lectio divina*, see Kay L. Northcutt, *Kindling Desire for God: Preaching as Spiritual Direction* (Minneapolis: Fortress Press, 2009), 145–46.

4. Justo L. González and Catherine Gunsalus González, *Liberation Preaching: The Pulpit and the Oppressed* (Nashville: Abingdon Press, 1980), 30.

5. Ibid., 84.

6. Wayne A. Meeks, ed., *The HarperCollins Study Bible, New Revised Standard Version* (New York: HarperCollins Publishers, 1993), 2202–3.

7. Paul J. Achtemeier with the Society of Biblical Literature, ed., *Harper's Bible Dictionary* (San Francisco: Harper San Francisco: 1985), 786.

8. Simon Hornblower and Antony Spawforth, eds., *The Oxford Classical Dictionary* (New York: Oxford University Press, 1996), 801.

9. Fred B. Craddock, *Philippians* (Louisville, KY: Westminster John Knox Press, 1984), 37.

10. Ibid., 35-36.

11. Ibid., 36.

12. Ibid., 38.

13. The basic outline of the Philippians letter comes from the *Harper's Bible Commentary* (San Francisco: Harper San Francisco, 1988), 1221–22.

14. Meeks, *The HarperCollins Study Bible*, 2205.

15. Harry Eskew and Hugh T. McElrath, *Sing with Understanding: An Introduction to Christian Hymnology*, 2nd ed. (Nashville: Church Street Press, 1995), 63.

16. Meeks, *The HarperCollins Study Bible*, 2206.

17. Craddock, *Philippians*, 39.

18. Caroline M. Noel, "At the Name of Jesus," in *The United Methodist Hymnal* (Nashville: The United Methodist Publishing House, 1989), 168. The hymn is also found in many other standard hymnals.

19. Craddock, *Philippians*, 36.

20. Ibid., 41.

21. González and González, *Liberation Preaching*, 50.

22. Ibid., 78–79.

23. Martha L. Moore-Keish, "Sixth Sunday in Lent, Philippians 2:5–11, Theological Perspective," in *Feasting on the Word*, Year B (Louisville, KY: Westminster John Knox Press, 2008), 170.

24. Ibid., 172.

25. Ibid., 172.

26. Craddock, *Philippians*, 43.

27. Pheme Perkins, "Philippians," in *The Women's Bible Commentary*, ed. Carol A. Newsom and Sharon H. Ringe (Louisville, KY: Westminster John Knox Press, 1992), 344.

28. Thomas G. Long, *The Witness of Preaching*, 2nd ed. (Louisville, KY: Westminster John Knox Press, 2005), 86.

29. Ibid., 86-91.

THE SERMONS PEOPLE RECEIVE

If we think of a sermon solely as what the preacher creates and delivers, we will have an entirely too narrow understanding of how preaching operates in the hearts and minds of a congregation. Everybody brings to the act of listening a personal history, a network of memories and associations through which they filter and process what the preacher says. The final result is that the sermons people receive are never precisely the sermons that preachers deliver. This is why many homileticians have reminded us how important it is to stay close to the "folk cultures" of our congregations in the preaching event. Henry Mitchell, for example, calls for a reclamation of the role of the congregation in terms of the language and imagery we use in preaching so that preaching stays closer to the ground of its hearers.[1] In *The Hum*, Evans Crawford talks about the ways in which the congregation itself is highly participative in the very act of preaching in many African-American churches through call and response. The congregation actually helps the preacher preach the sermon. Crawford reminds us that preaching isn't just the preacher's job; it is the church's job as well.[2]

On another front, scholars such as Lucy Rose and John McClure have been raising questions about the divide that occurs between pastor and people when the preacher assumes a kind of sovereign position above the listeners. Preaching, they claim, should be a collaborative act in which the preacher and congregation together co-create the sermon by gathering around the Word round-table style. In their understanding, the sermon continues to develop long after the preacher has finished speaking as the members of local faith communities mull it over, decide whether or not they believe it, and refine it for their own lives. It is especially important in the process of sermon preparation to include the voices of people who are marginalized so that their perspectives, too, become a part of what is brought into the pulpit.[3]

The development of a more communal understanding of preaching was anticipated in the 1960s by the pastoral theologian Reuel L. Howe.[4] He used the concept of "dialogue" to explore how sermons function in the hearts and minds of individual listeners as well as in the congregation as a whole. He came up with a sophisticated schema for diagramming the transaction that takes place between preacher and congregation. In what follows, I (Tom) am heavily indebted to Howe's original work, but I am updating his principles and charts in light of contemporary homiletical scholarship.

Howe observed that every time a sermon is preached, there are in fact three sermons: the preacher's, the listener's, and the congregation's as a whole. The preacher's sermon is the sum total of everything the preacher says and does. It includes the content of the sermon, but much more than that. It also includes how the voice, face, and body are used. These are all essential to understanding how the preacher communicates. Sometimes the voice, face, and body contradict the words the preacher speaks. The sermon is about the grace and peace of Christ, but the body is tight with strain, the voice punches the air, and the face has an angry expression. Grace may be spoken, but it is not received through the sermon. But there is also the wonderful possibility that the message and its embodiment will be fully integrated in the preacher so that the very manner of delivery gives witness to the truth of the words. The principle to keep in mind here is that the sermon is not what is written on the preacher's manuscript or stored in the preacher's heart. Of course, that is important. But it is only part of the sermon. To repeat: the preacher's sermon is the sum total of everything the preacher says and does. And the preacher's doing extends before and after the sermon is over. Does the preacher live what the preacher proclaims? That, too, is a part of the preacher's sermon.

The second sermon is the sermon that is received, processed, and created in each individual listener, and this sermon is never exactly the same as the preacher's sermon. Listeners respond to words, facial expressions, and physical gestures in different ways. Some of these varied responses are shaped by the listener's cultural background and family upbringing. Others are fed by unique personal experiences that have left an indelible impression upon the individual. The preacher has no control of these matters. Over the years, many preachers have told me a story that takes the same pattern again and again: they spoke on a particular topic, and a listener afterwards declared it to be a wonderful sermon about something the preacher never once mentioned or remotely suggested! Each listener receives and processes the sermon in her or his own way and, out of that complex mental and emotional action, creates a sermon of his or her own.

The third sermon is the impact of the preacher's sermon on the congregation as a whole. For example, a preacher may have spoken so persuasively about a need in the community that the sermon inspires the church to establish a significant new ministry. That response is more than each individual's sermon. It is the church's sermon as the corporate body of Christ.

This three-sermon model of preaching makes it clear that the preacher's sermon is not an end in itself. Instead, "The minister preaches his [or her] sermon *in order that* other sermons may be brought into being in the congregation, sermons that will be the joint products of both his [hers] and the congregation's effort."[5] Howe asserts that in order to awaken other sermons, the preacher needs to connect with the worlds of purpose and significance that lie within the listeners. When a sermon does not work, it is because it has failed to engage the way the congregation makes sense of the world. For Howe, one of the essential questions for a preacher is: What are the barriers to meaningful communication and how can I overcome them?

In the following table, I have drawn upon Howe's work but have substantially modified it in light of recent theological and homiletical developments, and especially, the suggestion of Henry Mitchell, who, at a meeting of teachers and scholars of homiletics, insisted that a sermon needs not only to engage meaning but also "to empower" people to live their faith.

surface barriers to
meaning and empowerment

language
images
appearances
cognitive development

2	**3**	**1**
Each Individual's Sermon as They Receive and Process	The Church's Sermon	The Preacher's Sermon

deeper barriers to
meaning and empowerment

differences
anxieties
defensiveness
culture
histories[6]

Howe's insights are helpful in understanding the active role of the congregation in creating meaning. Even our most finely crafted, theologically sound, beautifully illustrated, engaging sermons will be received and understood in different ways by different listeners. If you are in a group that offers you feedback about your preaching and people are offering very different versions of what they heard, remember this diagram. Do not become defensive and argue with them, saying, "But that is not what I said," for whether or not you said it, their version tells you what they did with your sermon, the way they received and processed it, the way they created meaning from everything you did and said. This does not imply that homiletics is reduced to the individual subjectivity of every listener. Remember sermon 3, the church's sermon. After teaching homiletics for many decades, we can both attest to the powerful impact excellent sermons have on a congregation as a whole. Whether in class or in church or at conferences, we have again and again heard sermons that drew everyone into a living encounter with the word of God, the Holy Spirit, and the living Christ, and although each person had her or his own perspective on the sermon, all felt the meaning and empowerment that the sermon had for them as a group and not just as individuals. Effective preaching transforms and inspires both individual lives and the collective life of the community.

When a sermon does not go well, return to the diagram and ask what barriers to meaning and empowerment you failed to address or account for. Were the words you used or an image you employed a stumbling block for the congregation? Or were there deeper barriers to meaning, some anxiety on your part and that of the congregation because you were preaching on an explosive issue? The conclusion is not that you should avoid difficult topics and events, but rather that you want to think thoroughly about how you can deal with the anxiety, resistance, and defensiveness that may be awakened in the listener.

When a sermon does go well, you need to spend time naming the things you did right, celebrating them, and making them a resource for your future sermons. Most of us have been told that we should learn from our mistakes. It is sound advice, but only partial advice. We also need to learn from when we do things well. Studying our best efforts is essential to developing our most effective ministry as preachers. It will help us create and deliver sermons that awaken rich and nourishing meaning in those who receive and process them.

Exercise: Barriers to Meaning

1. Think of a sermon you have heard in which the preacher's message did not get through to you because either the surface barriers to meaning or deeper barriers to meaning were at work. Identify specific details while referring to the Reuel Howe diagram above.

   _____

   _____

   _____

2. Is there anything the preacher could have done to make a difference in how you received the sermon? It may be the case that the preacher could not have done anything to reach you because the barriers were in you. If that was your experience, what does it tell you about how much control a preacher has over how a sermon is received? On the other hand, if there were things the preacher could have done, what does that tell you about attending to the potential barriers between preacher and congregation?

   _____

   _____

   _____

Notes

1. Henry H. Mitchell, *The Recovery of Preaching* (New York: Harper & Row, 1977), 11, 24, 29.

2. Evans E. Crawford, *The Hum: Call and Response in African American Preaching* (Nashville: Abingdon Press, 1995).

3. John S. McClure, *The Roundtable Pulpit: Where Leadership and Preaching Meet* (Nashville: Abingdon Press, 1995), and Lucy Atkinson Rose, *Sharing the Word: Preaching in the Roundtable Church* (Louisville, KY: Westminster John Knox Press, 1997).

4. Reuel L. Howe, *Partners in Preaching: Clergy & Laity in Dialogue* (New York: The Seabury Press, 1967).

5. Ibid., 72, emphasis added.

6. An adaptation and modification inspired by Reuel Howe's diagram on p. 72 of *Partners in Preaching*, using insights from Kathleen M. Black, Henry Mitchell, David J. Schlafer, and Clarence Snelling.

THE ROLE OF THE IMAGINATION IN PREACHING

In common American speech, the word "imagination" is often used to dismiss something as unreal: "It's all in your imagination," we say, or "You're just imagining that." But "imagination" also has serious connotations. It is connected with empathy, with our ability to sense what others are feeling: "We imagine ourselves in someone else's shoes." Preachers frequently invoke imagination in their sermons, asking listeners to imagine a scene from the Bible or common life.

Imagination is also seen as the mental ability to integrate various perspectives and intellectual disciplines, to see the interrelationship of things that upon initial consideration may not seem connected. Effective preaching is an example of the integrative imagination in action because it involves making connections between ancient scriptures and contemporary experience. Sermon preparation draws together a diversity of disciplines: biblical studies, theology, history, cultural and psychological analysis, and critical attention to literature and the media. Paul Wilson, in his book *Imagination of the Heart*, likens what happens in the preacher's mind to the leap of electricity across a spark gap.[1] Preachers hold close to each other ideas that are as seemingly different as positive and negative electrodes, but their very juxtaposition produces the spark of insight that reveals connections we had not made before. Through the exercise of the integrative imagination, the word of God illumines our lives here and now.

Imagination is also viewed as the visionary power of human beings: their ability to dream new dreams and create new realities. Cultivating this gift in a congregation is one of the major ways in which preachers help individuals find hope and empower congregations for mission and outreach. Christ says that he has come so that we might "have life, and have it abundantly" (John 10:10). Individuals who feel fragmented and lost need a vision of the abundant life that Christ offers, the wholeness and vitality of being that come through faith. Congregations need a vision of what they can become and do, a vision that energizes them for living the gospel. Joanna Adams puts it this way: "If I had to sum up what the purpose of preaching is in a sentence, I would say that it is to help people see the events in their lives and in human history from God's point of view. Preaching reshapes the human imagination so that, even in an often hopeless world, possibilities for new life can be discovered."[2]

Preachers, then, cultivate the imagination for three primary reasons: to empathize, integrate, and envision. The practice of imaginative thinking enriches our ability to touch the depths of the human soul with holy wonder and grace.

The cultivation of a theological imagination in preaching is especially important in an era when the media is bombarding people with so many alternative images of reality on a daily basis. Who will engage the imagination for God if the preacher does not? Who will help people name God's presence in the world if the preacher does not? And who will help people see that God has a different vision for our world if the preacher does not? In his book *Joy Songs, Trumpet Blasts, and Hallelujah Shouts!* Carlyle Fielding Stewart identifies "imaginative insight" as being one of the four corners of the black preaching universe: "The creative development of ideas through imaginative insight is essential in an age where preaching is in 'competition' with so many other media. The preacher must be creative without being pedantic, insightful without being boring. Because preaching competes with so many other idioms in present society, the preacher must be in touch with the creative elements of his [or her] art."[3]

Imagination in Theological Understanding

In recent decades, theologians have turned to a consideration of the imagination as an essential capacity for our relating to God and responding to God's Word. In his book *Imagining God*, Garrett Green revisits the early twentieth-century debate between Karl Barth and Emil Brunner over whether there is a divine-human contact point left within us human beings after the fall—a debate in which Brunner left open the possibility for such a contact point while Barth maintained that sin had obliterated it. Green seeks to find a middle way between the two. He puts forth the view that to be created in the image of God is to have the capacity to "imagine God rightly." What was lost to us in the fall was not the formal capacity to imagine—a faculty we humans still possess—but the capacity to imagine God *rightly*. Instead, we imagine God idolatrously, and create false images in place of the true God revealed to us at creation.[4]

What has been restored to us in Jesus Christ, "the image of the invisible God" (Colossians 1:15), is the capacity once again to imagine God and God's relationship with the world rightly. It is through faith in Christ that the idolatrous imaginations of human beings can be transformed and right relationships with God and neighbor restored. One of the primary ways in which this saving revelation is mediated to us is through preaching. Thus, Green writes, "To save sinners, God seizes them by the imagination: the preacher places himself at the service of this saving act by the obedient and lucid engagement of his [or her] own imagination."[5]

Note that imagination in this understanding is not undisciplined fantasizing but an obedient and lucid engagement of our own minds as preachers. We use our imaginations in order to image God in faithful and engaging ways for our congregations, and our congregations receive our preaching through the faculties of their own imaginations.

Therefore, one major question for preachers becomes how you will develop your imagination as a vessel for the Spirit of God. Or, more specifically, how do you imagine God in ways that can connect with your listeners?

The influential reformer John Calvin (1509–1564) has an insight about self-knowledge and the knowledge of God that is very helpful in responding to that last question: "True and substantial wisdom consists principally of two parts: the knowledge of God and the knowledge of ourselves. But while these two branches of knowledge are so intimately connected, which of them precedes and produces the other is not easy to discover."[6] Sometimes we learn something about ourselves that illumines a truth about God who created us, and sometimes we learn something about God that illumines a truth about ourselves. But these insights are often intertwined in complex patterns so that even after acute self-reflection, we cannot easily say which came first and which produced the other. What we can say, however, is this: the way we hold such knowledge in our minds is itself an imaginative act, an act of envisioning our relationship to God. Consider, for example, two different but common images for God in the Bible: shepherd and wind. What varied associations and relationships these awaken in our imaginations! God as shepherd suggests God's watchfulness, protection, and care. God as wind suggests God's energy, breath, and enlivening presence. How we imagine our relationship to God has a significant impact on our preaching, often shaping the content of our sermons and even influencing our vocal tone and posture.

Sometimes there can be tension between a preacher's and a congregation's dominant way of imagining their relationship to God. I, Tom, recall a preacher who saw God as "demanding" while the congregation tended to see God as "nurturing." Although the preacher was an effective speaker with well-crafted sermons, his preaching awakened an undercurrent of tension in many listeners that was largely attributable to their very different ways of imagining their relationship to God.

EXERCISE: IMAGINING THE INTERRELATIONSHIP OF THE KNOWLEDGE OF GOD AND THE KNOWLEDGE OF OURSELVES

The following exercise is designed on the basis of Calvin's insight about the interrelationship of self-knowledge and the knowledge of God. The exercise is based on how we imagine God, ourselves, and the relationship between us. The first two columns on the left contain an adjective and a noun for God. The second two columns feature an adjective and noun describing ourselves. The final two columns consist of a verb and a noun indicating something we need from God.

Image of God			Image of Self		Image of Relationship	
		your				
Eternal	God		believing	daughter	prays for	love
Flowing	Stream		thirsting	son	thanks you	for water
Kind	Lord		Lord	happy	child	gives witness
Heavenly	Mother		trusting	creature	hungers	for bread
Tender	Father		sinful	sheep	brims with	joy
Source of	Life		joyful	singer	offers	praise
Risen	Christ		anxious	follower	seeks	reassurance
Demanding	Sovereign		angry	rebel	wants	faith
Loving	Spirit		faithful	priest	needs	a word
Mighty	Rock		threatened	friend	asks	shelter[7]

Instructions

Circle one word from each column and then connect them with a line and you will have a prayer, an expression of your relationship to God. For example, "Tender Christ, your anxious creature wants reassurance." Or, "Eternal Spirit, your joyful child brims with praise." Of course, you have more than one prayer in you, but for the purposes of this exercise try to identify your most elemental prayer, the prayer that most consistently characterizes your relationship to God at this point in your life.

If you do not find the word you want in any of the columns, you may substitute your own. But it must be only one word. The search for the right word is a way of clarifying what is essential to you in how you relate to God. If you use only the words on the chart, there are one million possibilities! Those one million possibilities suggest the richness of the divine/human connection that lies at the heart of preaching. They also serve to alert us preachers to how important it is that we not limit what we have to say about God to the personal character of our relationship to the divine. The Bible, tradition, creation, and the experience, learning, and wisdom of others down through the centuries all give witness to a deeper, more expansive knowledge of God than any of us can claim for ourselves, no matter how vital our personal faith and experience. This does not mean personal faith and experience are unimportant to us as preachers. They are often the means the Spirit uses to call us into ministry and to animate our sermons with conviction and passion. The danger is that we may constrict ourselves to the landscape of our own hearts and reduce our preaching of the gospel to what we have experienced and what we believe. Part of the joy and power of preaching lies in reaching beyond what we have known for a word from God that expands the faith and understanding of ourselves as well as our listeners.

Further Reflections

In addition to its use for preaching, this exercise can also be helpful for us when we are leading congregations in public prayer. I, Nora, once went to a workshop with British hymn writer Brian Wren in which he invited all of us present to take one of the biblical images used for God (rock, fortress, shepherd, mother hen, living waters, and so on), to free associate other words that image brought to mind for us, and then to construct a prayer using our assigned imagery. The results were stunning! Not only did we hear God addressed in multiple ways in that room; our whole understanding of God was expanded and enriched as we were reminded of the myriad ways in which God relates to us and we to God.

Theologically and existentially, much is at stake in how we address and refer to God. Years ago, when our children were little, it was the practice of my husband and me to say prayers with them every night before they went to sleep. Prayer time was not only a time for talking to God; it was a time for us to debrief our children's days with them. One evening, as I was putting our seven-year-old daughter, Leonora, to bed, she told me she had had a bad day at school. We talked about the episode that had upset her for a while, and then I asked her, "Would you like to talk to God about it?"

"No," she replied.

Startled, I asked her why she didn't want to talk to God about what had happened. "Because," she replied, "God won't understand."

"What makes you think God won't understand?" I persisted.

"Because God is a boy and this is a girl thing. So God won't understand."

Distressed over my daughter's response (I was, after all, a feminist who was intentional about using inclusive language for God with our children), I asked her one last question: "And what makes you think God is a boy?"

"If God isn't a boy," she retorted, "then why do we talk about he, he, he all the time in church?"

If we as preachers and worship leaders want to convey a God that is bigger than any one image or set of images, then it is critical that we address God and speak of God in multiple ways in worship. To do so is not only more biblically and theologically faithful; it also opens the way for all of God's children to see that they, too, are created in the image of a God who loves and understands them.

Notes

1. Paul Scott Wilson, *Imagination of the Heart: New Understandings in Preaching* (Nashville: Abingdon Press, 1988).

2. Joanna Adams, as quoted in *Best Advice for Preaching*, ed. John S. McClure (Minneapolis: Fortress Press, 1998), 7.

3. Carlyle Fielding Stewart, III, *Joy Songs, Trumpet Blasts, and Hallelujah Shouts! Sermons in the African-American Preaching Tradition* (Lima, OH: CSS Publishing Company, Inc., 1997), 11–19.

4. Garrett Green, *Imagining God: Theology and the Religious Imagination* (New York: Harper & Row Publishers, Inc., 1987).

5. Ibid., 149.

6. John Calvin, *On the Christian Faith*, ed. John T. McNeill (New York: Liberal Arts Press, Inc., 1957), 3.

7. This chart, in a slightly modified version, first appeared in Thomas H. Troeger, *Creating Fresh Images for Preaching: New Rungs for Jacob's Ladder* (Valley Forge, PA: Judson Press, 1982), 23. For a case study demonstrating how a preacher's dominant relationship to God, when very different from the congregation's, may create obstacles to communication between pulpit and pew, see pp. 22–28.

THE WEEKLY SERMON PREPARATION PROCESS

Each semester in our introductory preaching course, we set aside one day on which we invite a panel, composed of the local pastors who help lead preaching groups for our course, to make a presentation to the class on their weekly sermon preparation processes. We do so in part because we think it is interesting for our students to see the diverse ways in which very competent preachers go about putting a sermon together in the hustle and bustle of their everyday lives in ministry. It is also comforting for students to learn that there is no "one right way" to put a sermon together, but that each preacher needs to discover a rhythm and a method that works best for her or him.

Nevertheless, before we turn to specific details of sermon preparation, it is important to name two general principles that underlie and sustain the particulars of any faithful creative process. These principles may seem self-evident, but they are very easy to forget when facing the pressure of a deadline. Charles G. Adams succinctly names a primary principle that precedes sitting down to write: "The first thing I try to do is to get in touch with Whose I am and Whom I preach, that I may be clear about who I am and why I do what I do."[1]

The second principle affirms the importance of starting as early as possible and allowing as much time as possible for the sermon to cook in the mind:

The proper shaping of a sermon takes its toll upon every preacher's time. Try as we may, it is difficult to side-step the thrust of this weekly demand. Some wisely reserve a strict portion of each day for sermon work. This regular privacy allows the preacher to store away what he will need later and to stir up what was stored away earlier. This storing and stirring is a basic rhythm for pulpit readiness. The storing feeds that silent, unseen process for which the subconscious is responsible; the stirring is to examine the stages of sermon growth in that process. Sermons grow from seeds planted in the soil of the mind and heart. Acted upon by the preacher's inwardness those seeds mature in accord with a timetable peculiar to circumstances and individual creativity.[2]

In her book *Birthing the Sermon*, Jana Childers invites twelve women from diverse theological traditions and racial-ethnic communities to talk about their own sermon preparation processes.[3] While some of the women preach from a lectionary, others preach thematically or focus on one biblical book for a season. While some work all week on crafting their sermons, others don't begin their writing until Saturday night. While some depend on music or art or good novels to inspire their creativity, others find that it is strenuous physical exercise, or taking a gentle walk, or talking their ideas out loud with a friend that spurs their own creativity.

Childers uses the metaphor of "birthing" to describe both the hard, strenuous labor and the joyful exhilaration that can accompany the gestation and delivery of a sermon. She reminds us that the metaphor is not a new one, but one that has deep historic roots and is reflected in a sermon John Calvin preached on 1 Timothy 4:6–7, in which he compared preachers to wet nurses. "The dissolute nurse wastes her energies and has no milk to give the child," he wrote. But "she who will work readily and will take food and sustenance along with her normal rest, she will be able also to feed her baby. So it is with those who have to preach the word of God."[4]

In this chapter, we have invited five of the pastors who have made presentations for our introductory preaching course to summarize their own "birthing a sermon" processes for you. As you read their reflections, we encourage you to think both about (a) what questions you would ask these preachers if you could, and (b) which methods and weekly rhythms of sermon preparation might work best for you.

Preparation Process #1: Pastor Andy

When I was a divinity school student, a professor urged us to plan our sermons a month at a time or by liturgical season. It's a fine idea. And there have been times in my fifteen years of pastoral ministry when I have looked ahead in the lectionary. But most weeks my process of sermon preparation begins on Monday morning.[5]

Monday: To begin, I become familiar with the assigned texts. I tend not to do any heavy exegetical work on Monday, but by day's end I know which text or texts I will focus on and I have begun to commit the text(s) to memory. This memorization allows me to "carry the Word" with me throughout the week. This is also the day to pick hymns and write parts of the liturgy for the coming Sunday. Frankly, that's often not done until Wednesday morning.

Tuesday: My day of rest.

Wednesday and Thursday: These are days of biblical study and extra-biblical reading. Days to walk-and-pray. Days to walk-and-think. Days to hike-and-pray-and-think. Time to be awake to possible connections between the congregation's life and events of the local, national, and international community; and events (of the local, national, and international community) and the text. I have described this part of the process as my Homiletical Net. It is as if I walk through the week with a net that catches this and that; the findings are relevant to the text I have memorized and often provide a direction or an illustration for my message.

Friday: Write. Since moving to Vermont, I have gone to the college library for sermon writing. In many ways, the writing is a synthesis of work already done. I tend to have a clear idea of what my message will be. My self-test: I try to write in one sentence what my sermon will be about. It's harder than it sounds. Once I have that in focus, my writing seems to be clearer and to come more quickly.

Saturday: In the evening, I memorize my sermon. My goal is not to recite the sermon the next morning. But I want to be so familiar with it that I could speak the sermon verbatim if I needed to. This familiarity with the preaching text allows me to feel more comfortable in the pulpit. I feel able to just preach it (!) and not rely on the words on the page. This prep time is essential, which is why I stay in most Saturday nights.

Sunday morning: I arrive at my study at church between 7:00 and 7:30, enjoy a cup of coffee, and look over my sermon and other parts of the liturgy. It's a still point. A centering time. I love that quiet. Hours later, when I stand in the pulpit, I want to see the people, and reach them, and move them from somewhere to somewhere else. When the sermon takes flight, I am reminded of

George Herbert's poem "The Windows," in which the preacher is described as "brittle crazie glasse" through which God's grace shines.[6]

There is much to say about how all of this happens. But I am regularly reminded of three things. First, I am impressed by how much pastoral visitation matters to the preaching process. To reach the people week after week, I need to really know them. Second, I am mindful of how much words matter. I try to choose them carefully and try to keep in mind the marriage of words' meanings and sounds. Third, I am weekly humbled by the Spirit's presence in the process of writing and delivering a sermon. I can't adequately explain or express this, but there are times each week when I sense that something more-than-me is the true author of my message. For all of this, I thank God.

Preparation Process #2: Rev. Bonita

Sermon preparation and delivery can be compared to bread making. The process is exact but involves creativity.[7]

The preacher should read the Word numerous times and check various translations. For me, this usually happens one week before I know that I am going to preach. I also make sure that a variety of other resources is available. They include but are not limited to a concordance, a Bible dictionary, a map, and a commentary. By Tuesday or Wednesday, I explore each of them, depending upon where my reading takes me.

The bread being prepared can include special ingredients to offer different textures and flavors. It is imperative for me to know the congregation and the context in which the sermon is to be delivered. I attempt to fit the sermon to suit the particular circumstances and environment. Use of the lectionary or observance of a special occasion in the life of the congregation might dictate one type of sermon. Another factor is a congregaton's cultural expressiveness or evangelical focus. All hearers do not like the same bread, so variety will help satisfy their diverse spiritual palates. I know to whom and the occasion for which I am preaching at the beginning of my preparation. This information guides me in adding the right ingredients mixed together in the right amounts.

I also have a strong desire to follow the direction of the Holy Spirit and the themes that emerge from listening attentively to the Spirit. Sometimes that happens during the process of preparation. Sometimes the revelation comes later.

The bread is best when the dough is given time to rise and bake slowly. I need to "let the sermon sit." This process involves reflection and prayer as well as conversation with others who have read or can offer commentary about the text.

By Thursday or Friday of the week I am preaching, I have selected at least three or four possible themes, working them through in my head and outlining the major points of the sermon on one page. I have constructed multiple sermons, during this process most of which I will never preach. This can, and regularly does, involve returning to the text for further review as well as reading other source materials to gain further clarity about the theme of the sermon. I want to be able to summarize the sermon's theme in one sentence. That way, I know I have internalized it.

The bread is most nourishing and enjoyable when served fresh. I often do not finalize the sermon until the night before. I review it and regularly make changes on Sunday morning. I am always surprised with what else, like butter or jam, gets added when the bread is hot. Applied in good portions, they add more flavor to the bread.

After all is said and done, my hope is that, as much as is humanly possible, the sermon speaks to what is happening within the community in which it is preached. It does not need to be perfect—in some cases, bread is best when it is not—but it does need to be edible. Fresh bread means that the word is fitly spoken, has a hermeneutical approach, and offers hope and good news for the living of these days.

Preparation Process #3: Pastor Julie

I have a love/hate relationship with preaching. I love it once I do it, but I often hate the "getting there" part. Sermon preparation can be so hard!

My own preparation process tends to have the following weekly rhythm:[8]

Sunday afternoon: Because I preach in a tradition that regularly uses the lectionary, I read next week's Scripture lessons after catching my breath from this week's sermon.

Monday: I reread the texts and also read them aloud. I take some notes on what the texts (and the Spirit) might be saying, a lead that I feel compelled to follow.

Tuesday: I check the exegetical background of the texts and the commentaries. Ordinarily I am doing so primarily to check on things for which I need clarification. However, on the weeks when nothing comes to me, I am looking for a suggested direction for the sermon!

Wednesday: I let things rumble around and settle. Do any images come to mind that might be useful for preaching this text? How can I make the Scripture come alive?

Thursday: It's time for me to write a rough draft of my sermon. I go jogging—which is always where I write and preach my best sermons. I then come home, light a candle, pray, and start in.

Friday: I finish writing the sermon. I might have to go jogging again. Then I put it away.

Saturday: I reread the sermon and practice preaching it, never before 5:00 p.m., never after 7:00 p.m.—unless I'm totally desperate.

Sunday: Before church, I practice it again. I do vocal and body warm-up exercises. And then, when the time comes, I give it all I've got, counting on the Spirit's help.

This is only the bare outline of the mechanics of my sermon preparation. What is more important is the daily life of prayer that undergirds and accompanies the mechanics, and the life of the congregation and the nation week to week. Personal, local, or national issues can sometimes change the direction of any sermon. But in all cases, I try to listen for the direction in which the Holy Spirit is leading so that by grace I may speak God's Word to God's people. It's fair to say that when the sermon works, it's because the text has worked me over and the Holy Spirit has had its way with me—and I have stopped worrying about whether it's "good" and worried instead about "am I speaking God's Word as best I understand it" to my congregation.

What do you do when you get to Sunday morning and know you have a bad sermon? Here I like to recount a response Nora Tubbs Tisdale offered in our preaching class one day when a student asked her what to do if you're in the midst of preaching a sermon and you can tell that it is not going well. She paused, thought about it a few minutes, and then replied, "Well, all I can say is, if you've got a dog, walk it proudly!"

Preparation Process #4: Pastor Ian

In my life, there is the ideal and there is the real process of sermon preparation.[9]

The ideal for me is to have a season-long overview of preaching in mind, to coordinate it with my associate chaplain and guest speakers, then to start serious exegetical/liturgical work two weeks in advance—composing the text of my sermon about four days in advance, and then revising it.

But in real life I have unexpected pastoral emergencies, weeks when I have five additional speaking engagements, or Fridays when I discover that I hate where my whole approach to the sermon is going. Sometimes—even on a Saturday night—a situation arises within the congregation that means I can't do what I had planned.

In a multi-staff, complex operation like University Church, where we plan our liturgies two weeks in advance and like to include our seminary interns and student musicians in worship planning, I don't have total freedom, nor do I want it.

There are a number of factors that affect my planning: Where are we in the academic calendar? What's the feel on campus this week? Where are we in the semester? Is everyone happy or crazed? Where are we in the liturgical calendar? How does my sermon fit in the flow of the season? Sometimes I find there is a lack of fit between the lectionary and the academic calendar (such as when the lectionary is offering up a series of sermons on tough parts of Luke and students are more in need of some pastoral care).

I photocopy the texts or have them on my iPhone for two weeks, carry them wherever I go, look at them, underline the verbs, and write questions and ideas in the margins. Then I use the *Feasting on the Word* commentary series and TextWeek.org to do the exegesis. I also look at what other good preachers and writers have done with the texts. Here I turn to a column in *The Christian Century*, blog sites, and especially John Shea's series *The Spiritual Wisdom of the Gospels for Christian Preachers and Teachers.*[10] In all these resources, I am looking for ideas and themes that combine some basic Christian teaching for the newer Christians in our congregation, as well as something that interests me. I assume that if an idea is intriguing to me, it will be interesting as well to other "old timers" who need a fresh perspective. I try to keep in mind my catechetical duties: am I covering basic theological ideas in any systematic way? I keep a list of basic areas that should be covered: creation, salvation, Christology, Christian anthropology, the Trinity, Christian social ethics, personal morality, and decision making, and I fill in gaps as I go.

While I don't have time to do it every week, I like to delve into early Christian sources just for a very different style—often analogical—of biblical interpretation. I also try to check in with the giants every now and then when I know a text matches: Fosdick, Beecher, Niebuhr, Tillich.

Writing: I need to do it all at one blow, pretty much. My ministry has a lot of complex, varied inputs and needs, and when I can find the time to get myself focused, I try to do a draft all the way through. This usually takes two to two and a half hours. Even if I'm planning to preach the sermon without a script, I write it all the way through, just because I need to see the logic and flow.

Then I revise it—ideally twice, but in actuality often only once on Saturday, or even on Sunday morning. I also practice delivering the sermon out loud—at least once as a part of the revisions, but ideally two or three times.

But I have one bad habit I can't shake: namely, writing one sermon, then thinking, "This is no good," and starting a second, related sermon, and then sometimes a third. Occasionally, I can take elements of the three and boil them down to a great sermon, but sometimes I end up delivering a mish-mash of the three that makes no sense.

Preparation Process #5: Pastor Shelly

Sermon Planning: My preparation begins as I plan my preaching themes a quarter at a time.[11] I take at least a day, sometimes more, to read through the lectionary texts for each week. I pray about what word needs to come to this congregation as I consider issues and themes. Then I select which of the lectionary readings we will read (we usually read two or three) and what theme I think I will follow. I also choose a sermon hymn. I keep a loose-leaf notebook with a page for each week with Scripture and theme written at top so I can write down ideas that occur to me throughout the weeks. I do this both for myself (nice to start each week with words already on a page!) and so that our music director can choose music consistent with the theme.

On **Monday** morning each week, I read the lectionary texts I have chosen out loud and then write a paraphrase of the text. I circle words that I don't understand or that jump out at me. If I have time, I do a word search or two or check the Bible dictionary for more information on a person or place.

Tuesday morning, I meet with an ecumenical group of colleagues to discuss that week's lectionary readings. It's amazing how many times over the course of a year my sermon will include the phrase "One of my colleagues said . . . ." In some churches, I have also had a Bible study with lay people during the week to explore the texts. It is a help.

Tuesday or Wednesday morning, I consult TextWeek.com and written commentaries (my favorites are the *Interpretation* and *Feasting on the Word* series). I pray and ponder both the text and the congregation and the news of the week in the world and tease out an organizing sentence for the sermon.

Thursday morning, I ask the secretary to hold my calls and visitors and I pray, then I write a first draft. I read the draft out loud and make any changes. Then I put it away.

Friday is my day off.

Saturday, I spend a couple of hours doing any major or minor revisions needed and I also speak the sermon out loud multiple times to learn it.

On **Sunday** morning, I arrive two hours before the service and spend one last time in revision and learning.

EXERCISE: SERMON PREPARATION PROCESS

Write down several questions you would like to ask these five pastors if you could. Discuss at least one of your questions with your peers.

_____

_____

_____

_____

_____

What do you think will be most difficult about the sermon preparation process for you? Most enjoyable? Most stretching?

_____

_____

_____

_____

_____

Notes

1. Charles G. Adams, "Preaching from the Heart and Mind," in *Power in the Pulpit: How America's Most Effective Black Preachers Prepare Their Sermons*, ed. Cleophus J. LaRue (Louisville, KY: Westminster John Knox Press, 2002), 13.

2. James Earl Massey, *The Sermon in Perspective: A Study of Communication and Charisma* (Grand Rapids, MI: Baker Book House, 1976), 90–91.

3. Jana Childers, ed., *Birthing the Sermon: Women Preachers on the Creative Process* (St. Louis, MO: Chalice Press, 2001).

4. Ibid., ix. The quotation is from John Calvin, "Sermon XXI sur la Première à Timothée." *Corpus Reformatorum*, ed. Guilielmus Baum, Eduardus Cunitz, and Eduardus Reuss (Brunsvigae: Schwetschke, 1895), vol. 53, col. 376 (Childers's translation).

5. Rev. Andy Nagy-Benson is pastor of Middlebury Congregational Church in Middlebury, Vermont.

6. George Herbert, "The Windows," in *The Essential Herbert*, selected with an introduction by Anthony Hecht (New York: The Ecco Press, 1987), 50.

7. Rev. Bonita Grubbs, an ordained minister in the American Baptist Church, serves as director of Christian Community Action in New Haven, Connecticut.

8. Rev. Julie Kelsey, an Episcopal priest, serves as Associate Dean of Student Affairs at Yale Divinity School in New Haven, Connecticut.

9. Rev. Ian Oliver is pastor of the University Church in Yale University and senior associate chaplain for Protestant life at Yale in New Haven, Connecticut.

10. John Shea, *The Spiritual Wisdom of the Gospels for Christian Preachers and Teachers* (Collegeville, MN: Liturgical Press, 2010).

11. Rev. Shelly Stackhouse is senior pastor of Church of the Redeemer (UCC) in New Haven, Connecticut.

EXEGETING THE CONGREGATION FOR PREACHING

Effective preaching not only requires us to exegete (that is, to interpret) biblical texts. It also requires us to exegete congregations and their contexts. As Teresa Fry Brown reminds us, "The preacher is the oral interpreter of the written text in the life *of a particular context at a particular time, for a particular purpose*."[1] Consequently, exegesis of the biblical text and exegesis of the congregation must go hand in hand. "We do not preach in isolation; [preaching] is a communal event."[2]

Exegeting congregations is important both pastorally and theologically. Pastorally, if we are going to preach effectively to a congregation, we need not only to come to know parishioners individually. We also need to know them collectively: who they are and who they have been as a faith community, their history, their culture(s), their hopes and dreams for the future, as well as their disappointments and struggles. As Eleazar Fernandez puts it, "To know the plight of a people, it takes more than a tourist acquaintance with their experience; even much more is needed to articulate their deepest pain as well as soaring hope."[3]

Theologically, we exegete congregations so that we can preach in ways that are both fitting and transformative for them.[4] To say that sermons are *fitting* is akin to what theologian David Kelsey is talking about when he says that theology, to be adequate, must be "seriously imaginable" for a particular people in a particular place and time.[5] When applied to preaching, this means that the theology of the sermon must make sense of life and faith for people living in a particular sociocultural and historical context. Exegeting the congregation helps us become more aware of the cultural worlds our congregations inhabit so that we can speak a meaningful and relevant word in their midst.

However, preaching does not simply leave congregants where we find them. We are also called to proclaim the gospel in such a way that its transformative power changes lives, reorients priorities, and brings about conversion in life and in faith. Therefore we also exegete congregations in order to learn more about what our people already believe, thereby gaining a better understanding of what it is about their life and faith that is in need of God's *transformative* word.

Ultimately, we exegete congregations because the Christian faith is, in its very essence, an incarnate faith, so our preaching must follow suit. As Robert Fukada rightly observes, "The preaching of the Word of God is valid and effective only when it is based upon a maximum comprehension of the cultural and social context, as well as religious orientation and needs, of the people to whom it is addressed. When we say that Christianity is a historical religion, with people living in a historical setting and time, we mean that the religion is rooted in a certain situation, place and time."[6]

Exegeting the congregation is not something about which I, Nora, received much training in seminary. It was assumed I would pick up this skill by osmosis once I started serving a congregation. But when I went out to serve in my first parish—four small churches in central Virginia—I realized I was going through culture shock not unlike that which I had previously gone through while serving as a volunteer missionary in a foreign country. One of the places where I first felt it was in my preaching.

For example, I remember referencing a contemporary novel in one of my sermons and sensing that the illustration fell flat. The urban worldview portrayed in the novel was simply too far removed from the worldview of my rural Virginia congregations to be "seriously imaginable." I also remember quoting theologian Karl Barth in a sermon one Sunday and having a parishioner come out the door saying that she'd heard me do many unusual things in my preaching, but this was the first time she'd heard me quote Karl Marx! What became clear to me upon further reflection was that the name Karl Barth made no sense at all in her world, and so, assuming she had misheard me, she substituted a name she did know, Karl Marx, for Karl Barth. Over time, I came to believe that the very structure of some of my sermons was off-putting to some of my less-than-college-educated parishioners, especially sermons that sounded overly academic in style and tone. And I consistently marveled at the different responses I would receive when I took the same sermon and preached it in four different congregations, all located within a fifty-mile radius of one another.

The questions these experiences elicited were ones I took with me into writing my first book, *Preaching as Local Theology and Folk Art*. I sought both to provide a method for exegeting congregations and their cultures, forged in conversation with the fields of congregational studies and cultural anthropology, and to reflect upon the significance of such exegesis for preaching.

My own approach is to focus upon some of the key signs and symbols of congregational life in order to see what they can tell us about congregational worldview, values, and ethos. By so doing, we also become more deeply aware of the "local theologies" people in faith communities hold dear. While not all of the symbols will be equally helpful in every context, investigating more than a few of them will give the preacher a more holistic and multi-faceted understanding of congregational life.

Below are two worksheets that can assist you in reading and interpreting congregational culture or cultures, as many congregations have multiple cultures within them. The first worksheet, entitled "Seven Symbols for Congregational Exegesis," identifies seven symbols that can be revelatory of congregational identity. The second worksheet, entitled "Interpreting the Symbols of Congregational Life," provides theological categories for reflecting on what you discern through your study of key congregational symbols about worldview, values, and ethos.

Please read through both, and then engage in the exercise that follows.

Seven Symbols for Congregational Exegesis

1. Congregational Narratives and Stories[7]

Who emerge as heroes in congregational stories, and what are the qualities that have made them so? Who emerge as villains, and what are the characteristics that have made them so?

Where are the silences in the storytelling of the congregation, the things many "insiders" know but few will talk about? What do they tell you about congregational identity?

Are there any recurring images or metaphors in the congregational story as people tell it that give you insight into how they perceive themselves and their world?

Is there any common dream or vision that seems to unite this people as they move toward the future?

If you were to plot the story of this congregation like the plot of a novel, what would that plot line look like? If you were to compare this congregation's story with another well-known story or myth (a biblical story or other story), to what would you compare it?

2. Rituals of Congregational Life

What is distinctive about the congregation's worship practices? What parts of the order of service are highlighted and seem to hold particular meaning for the congregation? What parts are de-emphasized? Are there any common theological themes you discern in hymns, prayers, sermons, or anthems that give you clues about congregational identity?

In the yearly cycle of this congregation's life together, what holidays or holy days are most significant, and how are they celebrated?

What annual, monthly, or weekly ritual practices are somewhat unique to the practice of this congregation (for example, a weekly service at a local nursing home, a monthly service for healing, an annual "All Saints Day" service of remembrance)? What do they tell you about congregational identity?

What "rites of solidarity," rituals that help unite communities by reminding individuals of what they have in common, and what "rites of passage," rituals that mark a significant change in the lives or roles of individuals within the community, are regularly practiced in the life of the congregation?

3. Art and Architecture

What is communicated about this congregation by the placement and design of its building?

How is the internal space used, arranged, and decorated? Is any part of the building "owned" by a particular group within the church? What messages are communicated through bulletin boards, posters, plaques, and so on that hang on the walls? What priorities are communicated by the way space is assigned? Can newcomers easily find their way around the building?

What do you learn by the art, architecture, furnishings, and spatial arrangements of the church sanctuary?

4. People

Who are the people the congregation considers its "sages," and what makes them so?

Who are the people who seem to be living "on the margins" of congregational life, and why?

5. Events

What types of events or activities receive the most attention, time, energy, and investment of resources (people and money) in congregational life? What types of activities are relatively under-emphasized?

Of which activities/events do congregation members speak with greatest pride and enthusiasm?

Which activities/events have stirred up the greatest controversy, and why?

6. Website Information, History, and Archival Materials (This is often a great place to start your research.)

What do you learn about the church from browsing its website and reading any histories that have been written about the life of its congregation?

What does the church's collection of archival materials (documents related to its founding, minutes of its decision-making bodies, financial records, printed and website materials) tell you about its past and present identity?

7. Demographics

What is the current demographic makeup of the congregation in regard to age, gender, race, ethnicity, social class, and so on? How would you describe a "typical" member? Who is noticeably absent?

How do these statistics compare with statistics from the past? With the church's perception of itself in the present? With the church's vision for itself in the future? With national congregational statistics? With the makeup of the community surrounding the church?

Interpreting the Symbols of Congregational Life

1. View of God[8]

Is God primarily imminent or transcendent?

Is God primarily law giver or grace giver?

Is God the sender of tragedy, powerless to stop it, or present with people in it?

What metaphors for God, for Christ, and for the Holy Spirit are most prevalent in congregational life?

Which person of the Trinity is least emphasized? Most emphasized? Absent?

2. View of Humanity

What is the predominant congregational view of human beings and human nature?

How do people see themselves in relation to the rest of society? as powerful or powerless? as change agents or victims of circumstances?

What does this congregation value in human nature: being, doing, or becoming?

3. View of Nature

Is the congregation's basic stance toward nature one of harmony with nature and the cycles of the seasons? mastery over nature? subjugation to nature?

4. View of Time

Is time primarily something to be managed and used efficiently, something to be endured (as in "doing time" in the prison), or something viewed more relationally (things begin when the community gathers)?

Is the congregation primarily oriented toward the past (tradition is all important), the present (living for today), or the future (actively planning for change)?

What is the character of congregational "hope," and how is it related to biblical images of hope such as "eternal life," "end times," "heaven and hell," or "resurrection"?

5. View of the Church

What metaphors for the church predominate in congregational life (for example, church as family, as sacramental community, as place of belonging, as mission and outreach organization, as prophetic presence in the city, as herald of good news)?

Is the church primarily seen to be a hospital for sinners or a holy community of saints?

How inclusive is the congregation of those who are frequently marginalized in larger society?

6. View of Christian Mission

How might the congregation be characterized in terms of its mission orientation?

a) Activist: emphasizing the corporate and public address of social, political, and economic issues?

b) Civic: emphasizing individual action on public issues, undergirded by church-based study and reflection?

c) Evangelistic: emphasizing the call of individuals to salvation and eternal life?

d) Sanctuary: providing a "haven in a heartless world"?

7. View of Sin, Evil, and Salvation

How does the congregation account for the presence of evil in the world, and in their individual lives?

What is considered to be sinful in this congregation, and what is not?

What is salvation, and how is it effected in our lives?

Is the primary emphasis in the congregation on personal conversion? Nurturing people into faith? Living ethically in light of faith? Sanctification through the Spirit?

A Case Study

I, Tom, have often found myself using Nora's tools for interpreting a congregation's life and values. Churches regularly commission me to write a hymn text to celebrate the anniversary of their founding or some other special occasion, such as the retirement of a beloved pastor or the installation of an organ or the dedication of a new building. Creating a hymn text for a particular congregation is like creating a sermon for a particular congregation: it requires understanding what Nora terms "their local theology." The local theology becomes even more significant on special celebrations, because it shapes and frames the meaning of the occasion for the congregation.

In most cases, I have never attended the church that commissions me, so initially I know nothing about their history and ministry. The first step in providing them with a hymn text that will be meaningful to them is to exegete the congregation. I usually get a start by visiting their website, but nothing can replace what Nora calls "congregational narratives and stories," a category that includes "recurring images or metaphors." I think, for example, of a church that commissioned a hymn to celebrate their past while looking to the future. I had a long-distance phone conversation with the committee overseeing the church's special celebration. I had taken extensive notes. Coming to the end of the conversation, I asked if there was anything else that might be helpful to my writing a hymn for them. There was a long pause, and then someone said with embarrassment in his voice, "I know this probably sounds corny, but several of us thought we ought to tell you about the cross, a very special cross, but then thought you might find it a little too lightweight." The committee then proceeded to tell me that several years ago a building next to the church had erected a structural element on its roof that involved a vertical tower and horizontal beam. At certain times of the year, when it was a sunny Sunday, the structure cast the shadow of a cross through one of the church's large windows onto the Lord's table, and this happened not infrequently when they were having communion! Although they understood it to be happenstance, they still found it profoundly moving. I could tell from their voices that this fortuitous phenomenon was filled with meaning for them, and I told them I did not consider it "corny" at all. Relieved at my response, they went on to tell me how important the shadow of the cross was to their worship and prayer, and as a direct result of that conversation, I wrote the opening stanza for their celebratory hymn:

> Where the cross still casts its shadow
> there we trace love's depth and height
> pouring forth to bless and hallow
> our own lives with that same light
> which through every twist and turning
> of our church's early days
> helped our founders in discerning
> how to serve the God they praised.[9]

They were delighted that I got the shadow of the cross into their hymn. It was the same delight that fills listeners when a preacher connects deeply to the congregation's local theology.

The story illustrates why it is important to exegete the congregation, why it matters to ask "What do you learn by the art, architecture, furnishings, and spatial arrangements of the church sanctuary?" I would never have found out about the shadow of the cross if it were not for the member of the committee who dared to risk what he feared I might find "corny" but shared what mattered mightily to him and the whole committee. It is this kind of making connections between the preacher and the people that we aim for in exegeting a congregation.

To get you started in developing your ability to exegete a congregation, we invite you to engage in the following exercise.

EXERCISE: CONGREGATIONAL EXEGESIS

Identify one of the seven symbols that is significant in the life of a congregation you know well. Provide a description of it below.

1. What does the symbol communicate about the congregation's worldview, values, ethos, or local theology?

_____

_____

_____

2. If you were the pastor of this congregation, how might the congregation's own local theology—as evidenced through the symbol you have identified—influence how you preach to them?

_____

_____

_____

3. If in a group setting, discuss your answers with three other people, and then with the group as a whole.

_____

_____

_____

Notes

1. Teresa L. Fry Brown, "The Action Potential of Preaching," in *Purposes of Preaching,* ed. Jana Childers (St. Louis, MO: Chalice Press, 2004), 52. Italics added for emphasis.

2. Ibid., 57.

3. Eleazar S. Fernandez, "A Filipino Perspective: 'Unfinished Dream' in the Land of Promise," in *Preaching Justice: Ethnic and Cultural Perspectives,* ed. Christine Marie Smith (Cleveland, OH: United Church Press, 1998), 62.

4. For more detailed information on how to exegete congregations and preach in ways that are fitting and transformative for them, see Leonora Tubbs Tisdale, *Preaching as Local Theology and Folk Art* (Minneapolis: Fortress Press, 1997).

5. See David H. Kelsey, *The Uses of Scripture in Recent Theology* (Minneapolis: Fortress Press, 1975), 170–74.

6. Robert Mikio Fukada, in *Preaching as God's Mission,* ed. Tsuneaki Kato (Tokyo: Kyo Bun Kwan, 1999), 194.

7. The material in this worksheet is a composite and expansion of material that is included in *Preaching as Local Theology and Folk Art,* pp. 64–77.

8. The material in this worksheet is a composite and expansion of material that is included in *Preaching as Local Theology and Folk Art,* pp. 80–86.

9. Thomas H. Troeger, *Above the Moon Earth Rises: Hymn Texts, Anthems, and Poems for a New Creation* (New York: Oxford University Press, 2002), 78.

THE USE OF MULTIPLE INTELLIGENCES IN PREACHING

The human creature has an astonishing number of different ways to receive, process, and respond to the world, or to put the matter another way, people have multiple capacities for learning and knowing. Howard Gardner has developed a scientific understanding of these varied abilities called "the theory of multiple intelligences."[1] It is a helpful tool for preachers because it suggests how to reach people on the spectrum of different ways of knowing that are present in most congregations.

According to Gardner, people possess eight different intelligences. Each one has a biological basis and is located in a particular region of the brain. If that region is somehow injured, a person will lose some or all of that intelligence. For example, a stroke will commonly restrict an individual's capacity to use words.

Assuming there is no disabling condition, all of us have all eight intelligences, but depending upon the culture in which we are raised and the kind of education we receive, most of us develop some intelligences to a more sophisticated level than others. Preachers, for example, tend to have highly developed verbal intelligence because their ministry requires the effective use of language. In a similar way, basketball players have developed their bodily intelligence, architects their visual intelligence, physicists their mathematical intelligence, composers their musical intelligence, and so forth. Although certain intelligences may dominate in particular fields of human endeavor, it is important to remember that the others are still present and can be developed. This is important for us preachers to know because it points to our need to use a repertoire of different ways of knowing in our preaching. I, Tom, have often been delighted after drawing on an example from science or math or music in a sermon to have a scientist or a mathematician or a musician engage me in conversation at some length. Each time, they begin by speaking about the point in my sermon where I had engaged their strongest intelligence. My acknowledgement of their primary way of receiving, processing, and responding to the world became a bridge of communication that allowed them to enter more fully into the world created by the sermon. I have come to understand that we preachers need to employ a repertoire of different ways of knowing, "multiple intelligences," in order to connect with the multiple ways of knowing present in individuals and in the congregation as a gathered body.

This use of multiple intelligences in preaching finds solid theological grounding in the first and greatest commandment: "'Hear, O Israel: the Lord our God, the Lord is one; you shall love the Lord your God with all your heart, and with all your soul, and with all your mind, and with all your strength'" (Mark 12:29–30). Heart and mind and soul and strength are the Hebrew way of saying the sum total of your human creaturely being, all that God has made you, all that God has given you, including your multiple intelligences. By drawing on a wide repertoire of varied ways of knowing when we preach God's Word, we embody what it is to give the wholeness of who we are to God, and we honor the principle that "preaching is ministry that focuses on the head, heart, and soul of the individual."[2]

Here is a chart of the eight multiple intelligences that Howard Gardner has identified:[3]

Multiple Intelligences Chart

Linguistic (word smart) - are sensitive to spoken and written language - learn languages - use language to accomplish certain goals	Logical-mathematical (logic smart) - analyze problems logically - carry out mathematical operations - investigate issues scientifically	Musical (music smart) - have skill in performance - have skill in composition - appreciate musical patterns	Bodily-kinesthetic (body smart) - use one's whole body - use parts of the body (for example, hand) - use body to solve problems - use body to fashion products
Spatial (picture smart) - recognize and manipulate patterns of wide space (for example, pilots) - recognize and manipulate patterns of more confined space (for example, sculptors and architects)	Interpersonal (people smart) - understand intentions, motivations, and desires of other people - work effectively with others	Intrapersonal (self smart) - have capacity to understand oneself - have an effective working model of oneself - regulate one's life effectively	Naturalist (nature smart) - recognize and classify numerous species of one's environment - relate to flora and fauna

There are two ways preachers can use this chart in the preparation of sermons. First, they can keep it in view as they read through a biblical passage. Preachers tend to focus on the linguistic intelligence, giving close attention to the meaning of words and phrases, but this chart can help them become aware of how other intelligences are engaged by a biblical text. Such awareness requires a slow reading of the scriptural passage, taking time to imagine what sounds (music smart) might have arisen from the actions, what the posture or position of a character might be (body smart), what the equivalent of a biblical measure (logic smart) might be. In other words, the intelligence may not be specifically named by the passage, but in imagining the scene (picture smart), a variety of intelligences may be implicitly present in the passage. Sometimes, all eight will be engaged, but not always. The important point is that by using the chart, preachers often begin to see things in the text that previously had eluded them.

Second, preachers can use the chart to expand the repertoire of ways of knowing that they employ in their sermons. They can review past sermons to discover which ways of knowing they favor and which they neglect. Then they can make a conscious effort to broaden their repertoire so as to reach a wider range of listeners, aware that many of those "listeners" are using far more than their ears to receive, process, and respond to the sermon.[4]

Here is a condensed version of a sermon on Luke 24:13–35, the road to Emmaus story. It uses all eight intelligences to give you an idea of how the theory works out in practice. I have indicated in brackets [ ] when a particular intelligence is engaged, but there were also gestures and musical sounds that were part of my embodying the sermon that cannot be captured on the page: I walked in a dispirited way as I pictured the disciples walking toward Emmaus; I held my hands as though they were breaking bread when I told about Jesus breaking the bread [body smart]; I spoke with a depressed vocal tone when quoting the disciples' despairing comment, "We had hoped that he was the one to redeem Israel"; and, at the end, I used a contrasting tone of joyful affirmation for "The Lord has risen indeed!" [music smart].

I recall a cartoon I saw over forty years ago. The image leapt off the page and has stayed imprinted in my mind through all the passing years. But before I describe the image, let me tell you what was going on when I saw the cartoon because that will help you understand why it gripped my imagination [self smart].

It was the end of the 1960s. Some of you remember the '60s; others may have heard about the '60s from their parents or grandparents [people smart]. It was in the '60s that President John F. Kennedy was assassinated. It was in the '60s that his brother Senator Robert Kennedy was assassinated. It was in the '60s that the Rev. Martin Luther King was assassinated. It was in the '60s that the United States bogged down in a war in Viet Nam, a war that split our country viciously apart between hawks and doves. Three assassinations plus one war equaled four major events [logic smart] that defined a decade and fed the imagination of an artist whose cartoon continues to haunt me:

A lone human figure is sitting, slouched in a chair [body smart] in a room with two doors. One door says NO EXIT, the other NO ENTRANCE [picture smart]. NO EXIT, NO ENTRANCE. That is more than a cartoon. NO EXIT, NO ENTRANCE is a posture of the soul, a state of human despondency, a spiritual wasteland, the feeling of being trapped. NO EXIT, NO ENTRANCE. [music smart: the repeated phrase NO EXIT, NO ENTRANCE becomes a refrain, like the theme in a symphony. Also, word smart because it makes the sermon easy to follow.]

(I then describe in the sermon several examples of being in a state of NO EXIT, NO ENTRANCE: addictions, violent personal relationships, wars that go on and on, impoverished communities [people smart]; despair about climate change and toxicity in the soil and water [nature smart].)

After Christ's execution on the cross, his disciples were in a state of NO EXIT, NO ENTRANCE. We see two of them walking on the road to Emmaus. They are joined by a stranger; at least he appears a stranger to them. They tell their fellow traveler how they "had hoped" Jesus "was the one to redeem Israel" (Luke 24:21).

"Had hoped."

There is no two-word phrase sadder than that: "*had* hoped" [word smart]. Those weary disciples were in a state of NO EXIT, NO ENTRANCE. No exit from the oppression of Rome. No exit from the rule of violence and death. No entrance to hope reborn. No entrance to new life.

But then they invited the stranger into their home, and "He took bread, blessed and broke it, and gave it to them. Then their eyes were opened, and they recognized him" (Luke 24:30–31) [body smart]. All of a sudden, there was an exit. There was an entrance. Christ was the exit. Christ was the entrance. The two disciples ran back through the miles of night to Jerusalem to tell their friends Christ had appeared to them. When they arrived, their companions shared with them the same joyful affirmation that is ours today: "The Lord has risen indeed!" Christ is the exit. Christ is the entrance. Christ is the exit from a life of oppression, violence, and death. Christ is the entrance to hope reborn, to new life, to everlasting glory.

EXERCISE: USING MULTIPLE INTELLIGENCES IN PREACHING

1. Use the chart to identify how many of the multiple intelligences are engaged by a slow, imaginative reading of John 2:1–12. You can reproduce the blank chart below, and then write in where and how the text uses an intelligence.

Multiple Intelligences Chart

Linguistic (word smart)	Logical-mathematical (logic smart)	Musical (music smart)	Bodily-kinesthetic (body smart)
Spatial (picture smart)	Interpersonal (people smart)	Intrapersonal (self smart)	Naturalist (nature smart)

2. If you have already preached two or three sermons or you are preaching regularly, review your sermons using the chart. Which intelligences do you tend to favor? Which do you need to cultivate more in order to reach a wider range of listeners? Remember to consider how you used your voice, face, gestures, and body in giving the sermon because these may engage intelligences that your words did not.

Notes

1. Howard Gardner, *Frames of Mind: The Theory of Multiple Intelligences* (New York: Basic Books, 1983). In addition to Gardner's groundbreaking work, we have found the following work, which features a preface by Howard Gardner, to be especially helpful to preachers: Thomas Armstrong, *Multiple Intelligences in the Classroom*, 2nd ed. (Alexandria, VA: Association for Supervision and Curriculum Development, 2000).

2. Teresa L. Fry Brown, in *Purposes of Preaching,* ed. Jana Childers (St. Louis, MO: Chalice Press, 2004), 55.

3. Definitions are from Howard Gardner, *Intelligence Reframed* (New York: Basic Books, 1999). The summation of "smarts" within the parentheses are from Armstrong, *Multiple Intelligences in the Classroom*, 31–33.

4. For a more extended discussion of the use of multiple intelligences in preaching, including sample sermons, see Thomas H. Troeger and H. Edward Everding Jr., *So That All Might Know: Preaching That Engages the Whole Congregation* (Nashville: Abingdon Press, 2008).

A Repertoire of Sermon Forms

We have been looking at multiple ways of interpreting experience and Scripture, figuring out how to make theological words come alive by using the senses, and writing and speaking in ways that are grounded in concrete reality. Now we want to consider how preachers utilize these methods and organize a sermon that is coherent and easy to follow from beginning to end.

We need always to remember that a congregation sees and hears rather than reads a sermon. The spoken word has some great advantages over the written word: the inflection, pace, and tones of the human voice make it a wondrously effective instrument of communication, as do facial expression, posture, and gesture. Preachers do not just create sermons. They perform sermons. We may rebel at that word "perform" because in our culture, the word usually means someone entertains an audience. The homiletical scholar Richard Ward tells us, however, that "the term *performance* comes from the old French *par* + *fournir*, which literally means to 'carry through to completion.' . . . What is it that we do when we speak the sermon we have written in the study? Do we not bring it forth to completion in the act of speaking it?"[1] No matter how well written a sermon is, if we do not perform it well, our preaching will falter. But if we use our voice and physical presence in a way that is fully congruent with the content of the sermon, our speaking will give wings to the words on the page.

Speaking, however, carries certain liabilities that writing does not. Unlike readers, listeners cannot go back and consider again the sentence that stumped them or the transition in thought that eluded them. Preachers have to give great attention to how they organize their sermons *for the ear*.

We also need a repertoire of methods for organizing sermons so that we do not put ourselves— or our listeners—to sleep. We need a repertoire because different individuals receive, process, and respond in a variety of ways. Using a range of homiletical forms is a way to recognize and honor people's multiple intelligences, the varied ways they learn and gain knowledge (chapter 9). Furthermore, the Bible itself uses multiple forms for communicating the word of God: poems, hymns, histories, myths, maxims, curses, blessings, dreams, visions, commandments, laments, letters, laws, prayers, prophecies, parables, genealogies, theological treatises, and gospels are all a part of our canon. The Bible gives testimony to a God whose word is revealed in a multitude of forms.

Outlines and Plots

How we conceptualize the form of a sermon exerts a tremendous influence on our creative process. Consider the difference between thinking of the "outline" of a sermon, and the "plot" of a sermon. An outline suggests a logical arrangement of points and sub-points, something like this:

I. First point of sermon
   A. Argument for the theme laid out
      1. Counterarguments refuted
      2. Restatement of major point
         a. illustration
         b. illustration
II. Second point of sermon . . . etc.

As a child growing up in the 1950s who went to church every Sunday, I, Tom recall listening to such sermons again and again. My mother and I on the way home would sometimes review the three points of the sermon. Later, after I was ordained, I had a parishioner who told me that when he was growing up, the first question that the pastor asked the confirmation class each week was, "What were the three points of the sermon today?" It was a widespread practice, and these logical outlines possessed some attractive features: the human memory finds it easy to remember things in threes, and such sermons, in the hands of a skillful preacher, often had a refreshing conceptual clarity that fed the congregation with an intellectually sound understanding of faith. It belongs in every preacher's repertoire of forms.

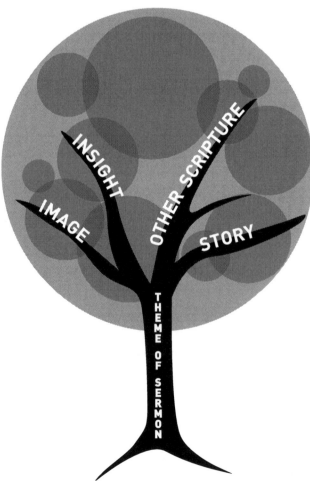

Cleo LaRue testifies that this form still works well in many African-American pulpits: "The three-point sermon in the black church is clothed in imagination, humor, playful engagement, running narrative, picturesque speech, and audible participation on the part of the congregation. Thus, it is not the three-point sermon that is out; instead it is the *boring* three-point sermon that must go."[2]

A variation on the classic outline of points and sub-points is the "trunk" outline, in which the preacher takes a phrase, verse, or image from the Bible and keeps periodically repeating it throughout the sermon. The trunk is the sermon theme. In between the repetitions, the preacher keeps adding "branches" to the "trunk": insights, stories, images, and other passages of Scripture that vary and illuminate the central point.

I, Tom, recall hearing a trunk sermon on the theme "God is a rock." Even though it is more than forty years ago that I heard it and I have listened to thousands of sermons since then, I cannot get the trunk out of my mind. The preacher started out saying, "The psalmist tells us God is a rock." He then dealt with all the forms of false security in which people invest their lives, repeatedly returning to the theme "God is a rock." By the end of the sermon, we felt the "rock-ness" of God, the utter dependability of God.

Because repetition is an effective form of oral communication, the trunk outline is generally easier to follow with the ear than the three-point outline, which leans heavily on logical, conceptual transitions. However, in light of the impact of electronic media, our growing understanding of the multiple ways people learn and know, and our greater appreciation of the range of literary forms found in the Bible, many homileticians nowadays find the "outline" form too static. It often lacks a sense of development and momentum, the kind of energy that engages a listener's sense of anticipation and curiosity about what is coming next. Outlines, particularly those with points and sub-points, are better suited for a printed essay than for oral communication. Such outlines are easy to follow with the eye, but they demand more attention from the ear than most people can give.

Gene Lowry has offered one of the most substantial critiques of building a sermon as an outline, and throughout this discussion we are drawing heavily upon his work.[3] Lowry observes that a sermon takes place in time. It is not like a building that occupies space, but more like music and cinema, and therefore, it makes more sense to talk about the "plot" of a sermon rather than its outline or structure. A sermon needs to move through time and carry the listeners along on the journey.

Instead of conceptual points, Lowry suggests a number of dramatic stages through which an effective sermon develops tension and momentum, as each stage flows toward the next. The first stage is "upsetting the equilibrium." The preacher describes a problem, a situation that is unsettling and whose outcome is not immediately apparent. Things are not right in Israel or in the life of someone who encounters Jesus in the gospel or in the experience of contemporary people. The situation, like the opening scene of a play or movie, draws listeners in. They are engaged, wondering what is about to unfold, and so they are ready for the second stage of the sermon, "analyzing the discrepancy": understanding why and how things go seriously wrong with life. Then comes the third stage, "disclosing the clue to resolution." The preacher brings the insight of the gospel, disclosing redemptive possibilities that the initial situation had blocked from sight. But the sermon does not end with only a clue. It moves on to "experiencing the gospel," to the sense of wonder, grace, and hope that rises in the heart through an encounter with the living Christ. Finally, that experience leads to "anticipating the consequences," to a vision of the implications for our living and embodying the gospel we have received.

Lowry has provided an interjection that captures the affect of each of these stages:

1. Upsetting the equilibrium (Oops)
2. Analyzing the discrepancy (Ugh)
3. Disclosing the clue to resolution (Aha)
4. Experiencing the gospel (Whee)
5. Anticipating the consequences (Yeah)

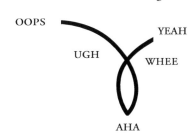

If you read the interjections aloud, it will give you an aural feeling for what has come to be known as the "Lowry loop," the way a sermon takes an unexpected turn as the gospel surprises us anew with the graciousness of God.

Moves

David Buttrick, like Lowry, has also objected to having points in preaching. He contends that speaking in points implies "a rational, at-a-distance pointing at things," an objectification that assumes that there are "fixed truths 'out there' to be talked about."[4] Instead, Buttrick argues, we need to think in terms of the movement of language and speech. When we converse with one another, we do so in a series of language modules put together by some sort of logic. There is a flow to our speech that needs to be replicated in our preaching. This insight leads Buttrick to propose a way of structuring sermons based on "moves."

According to Buttrick, moves are made up of the following three elements:

1. A theological understanding or idea
2. Oppositions (those things that block our understanding or embrace of the theology proposed; Buttrick calls them "contrapuntals")
3. The actualities of lived existence (Where in human life do we see this reality fleshed out? Where have we experienced it?)[5]

Buttrick provides the following example of a sermonic move:

We are sinners. *[opening theological statement]* "Sinners"—the word may sound old fashioned, but it's true: We are all of us sinners. Oh, nowadays we avoid the term. We say we have "hangups," or perhaps we rattle off psychological words [to explain our condition] . . . . *[He names and addresses the "contrapuntals"—our human opposition to seeing ourselves this way]* But again and again, we circle back to the old biblical word: We are sinners, all. Certainly, we can read about sin in daily papers. Big sins, murder or rape, are bold-type headlines. And certainly we notice sins in the lives of others. "She doesn't care about anyone else," we say, or "He's so vain." But when it comes to our own lives, how hard it is to see *our* sin. *[more contrapuntals]* Maybe sin comes to us in a brief, flashing moment of regret when we say to ourselves, "I should go back and apologize," but then we don't and the moment is past. Or maybe, it's when at tax time we flip through our check stubs and think for an instant, "I should have given more away." Or perhaps when we hear youngsters dream big dreams for their lives and we suddenly think, "Well, we've settled for less; we haven't been what we could have been." Then, we move away and try to forget. *[names the actual lived experience of when we know we sin]* Listen, the world isn't divided into sinners and nonsinners: Down deep we know our lives are compromised. "We're supposed to love," says a detective-story hero. "But we all flunk," he says. Sinners—that's the biblical word, and we know it's true. We are, all of us, sinners. *[restatement of opening theological theme/idea]*[6]

A sermon structure is composed of a series of moves, with an introduction and a conclusion. A typical structure would look like this:

Introduction: Makes a promise to the hearer about the nature and focus of sermon. Should clearly indicate the direction the sermon will take.

    Move #1

Connector: A connector could be a pause, a repeated refrain, a transitional phrase, a summary statement that completes one move and leads to the next, or a transitional story or example. Often, transitions are the most difficult parts of sermons to write, and if you find that you cannot find an appropriate connector to tie two parts of a sermon together, then the problem may lie in the logical flow of the sermon.

    Move #2

        Connector

    Move #3

        Connector

Conclusion: Generally, a conclusion should not introduce a new move or idea, but should complete the sermonic journey that has been taken.

I, Nora, have found that this mode of sketching out the flow of sermons can work with almost any sermon I preach. Even though my "moves" do not always follow Buttrick's prescription for them (I may, for example, use a narrative structure or a problem/resolution structure; see additional sermon forms discussed below), the whole notion of plotting the moves of the sermon before I begin writing it is one I find to be enormously helpful for making sure the sermon as a whole has a logical coherence and flow.

Principles to Consider When Choosing a Sermon Form

There are a number of very good reasons for you to develop a repertoire of sermon forms to use in your preaching ministry. In addition to the ones we have already named—that the Bible itself uses multiple forms of communicating, and that congregations and their members vary in the ways in which they receive and process sermons—it is also the case that variation in sermon forms is a good antidote to boredom and predictability in preaching. Many pastors I know have default forms they use when they write sermons, that is, forms they tend to use over and over again. In and of itself this is not a bad thing. We all need some trusted routines in preaching. However, it is also the case that over time, both the preacher and the congregation can become bored with sermons that are all structured the same way. Mixing it up not only helps us be more faithful to our multifaceted Bible and faith; it also helps keep our preaching fresh and new.

Furthermore, the structure of a sermon has theological implications. For example, a story sermon implies God is known through story, a logical argument implies God is known through reason, a sermon featuring personal experience implies God is known through personal experience. The fact is God is known through all of these and through many other ways as well. To settle for a single sermonic form is to constrict our understanding of how God is revealed. We not only communicate theology by *what* we say in preaching; we also communicate theology by *how* we say it. We need a repertoire of forms to be faithful to the God whose ways of revelation are broad and varied.

If truth be told, the only thing that limits the possibilities of sermonic form is the preacher's own imagination. Thus Choan-Seng Song reflects on the final words of the Gospel of John ("But there are also many other things that Jesus did; if every one of them were written down, I suppose that the world itself could not contain the books that would be written," John 21:25): "These striking words that conclude John's Gospel open up for us almost an infinite space of the story about Jesus. Nothing can exhaust that story except our limited imagination."[7]

There are, then, many diverse ways to structure a sermon, ranging from highly traditional outlines to more contemporary and experimental options.[8] However, it is also important to remember that in preaching, as in architecture, form follows function. The preacher should first decide what he or she wants the sermon to say and to do, the focus and function of the sermon (see chapter 6), and then develop a form that fulfills those aims.

Five Additional Sermon Form Options

In the section that follows, we present five additional sermon forms that have either been favorites of our own, or that are treasured forms in certain preaching traditions. This list is not meant to be exhaustive; rather, it is meant to be suggestive and useful for priming the pump of the preacher's own imagination.

1. Story Form: My Story, Biblical Story, Our (Congregation's) Story

The story form is used by many preachers in a variety of denominational traditions today. Lutheran homiletician and popular radio preacher of the mid-twentieth century Edmund Steimle describes this form in his book *Preaching the Story*.[9] The preacher begins the sermon by telling a story about something she or he has either personally experienced or has observed in everyday life, whether in person or through the media. The sermon then moves to a recounting of the biblical story, told in a way that lifts up and makes apparent the connections with the opening story. Finally, the preacher moves to the congregation's own story, drawing out the implications of the gospel story for the living of our days.[10]

Sermon Example: Edmund Steimle, "The Eye of the Storm"

A. My Story

"Hurricane Hazel sweeps through Philadelphia, and in the midst of the eye of the storm 'all was calm, all was bright.' And then all hell broke loose. . . ."

B. Biblical Story

"Christmas Eve is something like that, like the experience of the eye of the storm . . .

Mary . . . resting now, after the pain of the contractions and the delivery without benefit of anesthetic.

The child . . . sleeping peacefully in the swaddling clothes and the straw. At least we like to think him so."

But "make no mistake, he comes at the center of a storm—both before and after the birth. The storm before": Steimle here recounts salvation history from the flood of Noah through the Exile to the oppression of Roman occupation.

"And the storm after: The massacre of the innocent male children two years old and under by Herod in his frantic effort to deal with the threat of the child sleeping in the manger."

"What we tend to forget on Christmas is that these lovely stories of the birth . . . are not children's stories. . . . These are adult stories for adult Christians."

C. Our (Congregation's) Story

"We are aware of the confusion and destruction around us in the world. The violence in the Middle East, southern Africa and Northern Ireland, the hunger in the Third World. Or closer to home, the muggings on the streets, the unemployment (a grim passive kind of violence), the ghettoes, the injustice to the blacks, the inner cities gutted by poverty and inflation amidst massive indifference. . . .

"The point is, we don't forget this on Christmas Eve—or block it out. Like a person standing in the eye of a hurricane, we are aware of it all. If you want to forget it all tonight—OK! Go home and listen to Bing Crosby dreaming of a white Christmas. And there's a place for that—but not here!

"Christmas is not about forgetting the storm. Christmas is about peace pronounced in its very midst—'a peace that passes all understanding' because it is not a peace apart from conflict, pain, suffering, violence, and confusion. . . . it's a peace like the peace in the eye of a hurricane, a peace smack in the middle of it all, a peace that indeed passes all understanding. We rejoice in the hope born of the conviction that the storm, the destruction, the violence, the hopelessness, does not have the last word. But God—who gives us this 'silent night' in the middle of the storm—he has the last word."

Conclusion

"So rejoice . . . and sing the carols . . . and listen to the ancient story and light the candles . . . and be glad—with your families, your friends, with the God who is above all and through all and in you all, who comes to us miraculously in this child, this night when 'all is calm, all is bright.' "

2. Sermon Structured around an Image

The Bible is filled with images, and many of them can become a major metaphor that holds a sermon together. Think of the scores of sermons you have heard on Jesus as the bread of life, Christ the good shepherd and we the sheep, Christ the vine and we the branches, the church as the body of Christ. But the images do not have to be limited to the Bible. Most of us have picture galleries in our heads, memories of particular photographs, paintings, cartoons, favorite scenes from the movies, images from beloved hymns, poems and stories, and simple images from everyday life. All can be used effectively in preaching.

Prathia Hall builds on biblical imagery in a sermon she preached at the Hampton University Ministers' Conference titled "Between the Wilderness and a Cliff."[11] Hall begins her sermon by reminding us that Jesus' inaugural sermon in Luke 4 takes place between the "wilderness," where he was tempted by Satan for forty days, and the "cliff," where the people of Nazareth drove Jesus after he preached because what he said so angered them (Luke 4:28–30):

This is the context of Christian ministry. It is the context of our Lord's ministry. It is the context of Christian life. It is the context of African American life and struggle. It is the context of gospel preaching, and God in heaven knows it is the context of the ministry of women. We preach, pray, teach, heal, help, bless between the wilderness and then the cliff![12]

Hall then spends the major portion of her sermon recounting Jesus' experiences in wilderness and cliff and paralleling them with our own. The "wilderness" signifies the place where we, like Jesus, are tempted to surrender our identity and our calling. "The temptation of the cliff"—that place where people hostile to the message we preach try to push us—"is [to fall prey to] contempt for the crowd."[13] Hall calls us to resist both temptations, and to follow the way of Christ who, on the cross, took on both the wilderness and the cliff and won the ultimate victory over both.

On the other hand, Susan Sparks, pastor of Madison Avenue Baptist Church in New York City, takes an image from everyday life—a mulch pile where, through composting, our smelly garbage becomes good, rich soil for gardening—and uses it as an image for what the Apostle Paul is calling us to do with our anger, hatred, and malice in Colossians 3:8–10. She begins her sermon by recounting a trip she had recently taken to a cottage in Wisconsin, where her family, after consuming a large breakfast complete with cheese, eggs, blueberry muffins, and "fresh sunfish caught right off [the] dock," went out for the day. When they returned to their cabin—devoid of air conditioning and sweltering in the ninety-two-degree heat—the smell of the rotting fish and eggs was overpowering. Sparks recounts how she donned a gas mask constructed of paper towels and carried the garbage out to the mulch pile. She writes, "God bless mulch piles. For any of you gardeners out there, you know the magic of a mulch pile: a place where smelly fish carcasses and egg shells transform into rich, dark dirt; dirt that gives life to things like aromatic lavender and brilliantly colored day lilies."[14]

She then moves to the biblical text:

After fumigating the house, I sat down to read the lectionary scripture for the week to prepare for the sermon and saw our scripture in Colossians 3. Who knew there was a parallel in mulch piles and the words of the Apostle Paul? Perhaps he was a gardener? *"Get rid of all such things—anger, wrath, malice, slander, and abusive language from your mouth (the "trash") and clothe yourself in the new self."*

Two thousand years later, Paul reaches out and asks us all:

What trash (anger, fear, shame, jealousy) do you need to throw on the mulch pile?
And what beautiful new things will you grow in its place?

Sparks then gives an example of how a person might deal with anger by moving through the three stages of (1) "taking out the trash" (walking away from anger and getting some distance from it), (2) "throwing it on the mulch pile" (letting it go and handing it over to God), and (3) "beginning to grow something beautiful in its place" ("On the mulch pile, anger can become empathy, fear can become insight, pain can become strength").[15]

Finally, she moves in her sermon to assert that such actions work not only on the personal level, but also on the political level:

Consider the recent controversy over Park 51, the proposed Muslim community center near Ground Zero. There have been numerous protests, judgmental blogs and hateful radio and news commentaries bashing this idea. It will be a "Mega-Mosque," some say, "a Muslim extremist site."

As someone who was in NYC on 9/11, smelled the smoke from the crash, saw the second tower fall, I feel quite comfortable saying: "people—PEOPLE—throw it on the mulch pile!" This is nothing but fear talking; fear and ignorance that are stinking up our house. Take out the trash. Throw it on the mulch pile. Maybe then something beautiful will grow; something beautiful like an interfaith community center and worship space to honor the memory of 9/11.[16]

Note how Sparks not only gives us a powerful visual image for the transformation that can occur in our lives if we heed the apostle's advice; she also engages the sense of smell to show how the transformation of the "garbage" in our lives can, through God's work in us, give rise to fragrant flowers.

A third example of shaping a sermon around an image comes from a sermon preached by Mary Lin Hudson in the chapel of Memphis Theological Seminary titled "I Dream a World."[17] Hudson begins her sermon by recounting attending an exhibit at a local gallery where the photographs of seventy-five African-American women who had made a difference were hung. Some of them were well known: Coretta King, Oprah Winfrey, Leontyne Price. Others were not: Septima Poinsette Clark, "who believed that literacy was the key to empowerment," and who "developed innovative citizenship schools throughout the south"; Josephine Riley Matthews, "a licensed midwife who safely delivered more than 1,300 babies, black and white, in rural South Carolina"; Marva Nettles Collins, who founded the Westside Preparatory School in Chicago, where poor children were expected not only to learn, but also to serve their communities.[18] These women, Hudson observes, "dared to dream a world, and lived those dreams into realities through their courage and love."[19]

Hudson goes on to recount biblical and historical prophets, apostles, and saints—including the prophet Isaiah, the Apostle Paul, and Martin Luther King Jr.—whose portraits hang in "the gallery of our imagination" with an inscription under each that reads "Dreamer of Worlds." After quoting a portion of Martin Luther King's "I Have a Dream" speech, Hudson invites the congregation members to participate in her sermon by sharing their own dreams with one another: "I invite you to speak your dream aloud together right now and paint a picture of the world of our dreams. Call out your dream so that we can see it together. Begin your statement with the phrase, 'I long for a world where . . .' and those who wish to affirm that dream may respond with 'Amen.' "[20] She concludes her sermon with these words: "Hold fast to your visions. Keep on dreaming dreams. Let us move ahead into new creation and live toward the coming day of God's glorious peace."[21]

In her own commentary on this sermon, Hudson writes, "Instead of talking about prophetic vision, or explaining the purpose of these realities, I wanted the sermon to move people to listen to the prophetic voice within them and to find courage to express their ideas aloud. . . . The expression of visions was not just an imaginative act; it empowered the community to claim the new for themselves."[22]

3. Problem/Resolution

Harry Emerson Fosdick, the founding pastor of The Riverside Church in New York City and a highly popular preacher in the early twentieth century, regularly used the problem/resolution form to great effect in his own preaching. For Fosdick, the starting place for the sermon was nearly always a pastoral concern (such as loneliness, dealing with failure, or how to find meaning in life), a contemporary ethical issue (such as war), or a theological controversy (such as the fundamentalist/modernist debate) that he then explored and addressed from a biblical and theological point of view.

Sermons today might use this form to address ethical issues facing Christians (immigration reform, homelessness, the world health crisis), theological differences within the church (the debate over gay/lesbian ordination), or tensions that occur within the Bible itself (such as the tension witnessed in two opening stories in John's Gospel: the wedding at Cana, where Jesus turns gallons of water into good wine and appears to be the life of the party, and the second story, where Jesus is turning over the tables of the money changers in the temple in a holy rage. Will the real Jesus please stand up?)

Sermon Example: Harry Emerson Fosdick, "Shall the Fundamentalists Win?"

Problem
Fosdick describes the fundamentalist/modernist controversy, in which the fundamentalists maintained that science and Christian faith were incompatible, and modernists, such as Fosdick, maintained they were not.[23] He especially wrestles with the fundamentalist doctrine of the inerrancy of the Scriptures in matters of science by reference both to the virgin birth of Jesus and his second coming. He concludes this section of the sermon by asking the question "shall one of [these two opposing groups] drive the other one out [of the church]?"[24]

Resolution
In the face of intolerance on the part of the fundamentalists, Fosdick calls upon his modernist congregation to adopt two alternative approaches: (1) "a spirit of tolerance and Christian liberty,"[25] and (2) "a sense of penitent shame that the Christian church should be quarreling over little matters when the world is dying of great needs."[26]

Conclusion
"Never in this church have I caught one accent of intolerance. God keep us always so and ever increasing areas of the Christian fellowship; intellectually hospitable, open-minded, liberty-loving,

fair, tolerant, not with the tolerance of indifference as though we did not care about the faith, but because always our major emphasis is upon the weightier matters of the law."[27]

4. Thesis-Antithesis-Synthesis

Samuel Proctor, who taught preaching for many years at the School of Theology of Virginia Union University, has proposed a thesis/antithesis/synthesis structure, based on the Hegelian dialectic.[28] This form for preaching has been taught in a number of historic African-American seminaries and has been used to great effect by many outstanding preachers including Martin Luther King Jr.

The sermon begins by stating something many people assume to be true, the thesis. Then the preacher poses counterarguments to that thesis, the things that make us think it is not so true. And finally the sermon moves to a synthesis in which a more complex truth is revealed.

Sermon Example: Martin Luther King Jr., "How Should a Christian View Communism?"

Thesis: "Communism and Christianity are fundamentally incompatible."[29]
Arguments in support of the thesis:[30]
1. Communism has a "materialistic and humanistic view of life" and "provides no place for God or Christ."[31]
2. Communism "is based on ethical relativism and accepts no stable moral absolutes."[32]
3. "Communism attributes ultimate value to the state."[33]
4. Communism ultimately robs humanity of freedom and ends up with the human being as "little more than a depersonalized cog in the ever-turning wheel of the state."[34]

Antithesis: But communism also asserts truths that are consonant with the Christian worldview.
Arguments in support of antithesis:
1. Communism challenges the church—which has not been true to its mission, especially in regard to social justice and racial equality—to reflect Jesus' concern for the poor, the exploited, and the disinherited.[35]
2. Communism presses us to "examine honestly the weaknesses of traditional capitalism."[36]

Synthesis: The Kingdom of God is neither the thesis of individual enterprise nor the antithesis of collective enterprise, but a synthesis that reconciles the truth of both.[37]

5. Engaging the Congregation in an Experiential Activity

We know from our study of multiple intelligences (chapter 9) that one of the ways people learn is by processing reality through their bodies. Different cultures consider different bodily postures and gestures respectful or inappropriate. I, Tom, recently returned from a trip abroad where I was asked not to cross my legs because it was considered to be rude. I am so used to crossing my legs that for the first few days, I was crossing and then quickly un-crossing them. The habits that are inculcated in our bodies go to the marrow of our bones and are not easily changed. This is why engaging a congregation in a simple physical exercise or using our own body in a particular posture or gesture can be an effective way of creating and delivering a sermon.

For example, I recall a sermon from the 1980s by Sister Joan Delaplane on the woman bent double (Luke 13:10–17). She preached the first half of the sermon bent over and did not stand straight until she came to the part of the story in which Jesus heals the woman. That simple posture and gesture carried Delaplane's message home to my heart: we do not freely bend our back to anyone but God.

Sometimes the whole congregation is involved in the exercise. I once began a sermon by having the congregation pray the Lord's Prayer in their usual posture of sitting with hands clasped together, eyes shut, and head bowed. I then invited them to stand and take the ancient *orans* posture for prayer, hands lifted and open, head up, and eyes open, as they again prayed the Lord's Prayer. The sermon then went back and forth between the two postures, and the truth that is embodied in each of them. The clasped hands, bowed head, and shut eyes emphasize the interiority of prayer, the shutting out of the world's distractions, and finding God in the heart's deep core. The lifted and open hands, raised head, and open eyes embody an alertness to the world, a readiness to receive, and our need to be awake to the One who is coming. A full prayer life has room for both postures and for other postures as well, such as kneeling and prostration. Even when a posture is not taken by the body, it still can be taken by the heart and soul. However, what fixed the sermon in the congregation's mind was the actual experience of having been invited to offer the Lord's Prayer in both postures as part of the sermon. It was one of the sermons that I heard about for years after giving it. People would begin a pastoral conversation saying, "I am at a point where I need to pray like this," and then they would either bow their heads and shut their eyes or stand and lift up their hands. Engaging the bodily-kinesthetic intelligence had implanted the sermon in thought and memory so they could continue the work of prayer long after the sermon had been preached.

Using a simple experiential activity moves our sermons beyond words. It reminds us that the gospel is not simply talked about but embodied, that the Word we preach is incarnate. Here for example is the beginning of a sermon for Thanksgiving that tries to help us experience gratitude not just as a passing thought, but as an expression of our whole being:

I recently read that the human heart is about the size of our fist, and that on the average it beats one hundred thousand times a day. Make a fist with your right or left hand and start opening and closing it as if the fist were your heart beating to push the blood through your arteries and veins. [I wait in silence, opening and closing my fist for about fifteen seconds while the congregation is doing the same.]

Getting tired yet? Don't stop. This is your heart! [I stop working my fist to indicate the congregation can stop after all.]

If a heart beats one hundred thousand times a day, that means in a week it beats seven hundred thousand times. In ten weeks, seven million times. And if we multiply ten weeks by five we realize that in fifty weeks our heart beats thirty-five million times. But we still have two weeks to go to reach a year, and we have not allowed for all the times we went jogging or chased our cat or dog. So in round figures our hearts beat forty million times a year. That means by the time we are ten, our hearts have beat four hundred million times. By the time we are twenty: eight hundred million times. By the time we are thirty, ONE BILLION TWO HUNDRED THOUSAND times! I am well past TWO BILLION FOUR HUNDRED THOUSAND heart beats. What about you?

I have a simple question: have you ever gotten a bill for all these heart beats? I have never received a notice saying: "Mr. Troeger, you are sixty-seven years in arrears on your heart beat charges. Pay up now or we are shutting off service."

To exist is grace. To be born is a gift. We did absolutely nothing to earn it. The next time you are wondering what God has ever done for you, feel for your pulse, and with every heart beat say: thank you, thank you, thank you, thank you, thank you, thank you, thank you, thank you, thank you, thank you, thank you, thank you. [I hold out my arm and take my pulse as I speak and walk back to my seat repeating the final words.]

EXERCISE: USING SERMON FORMS

Choose any one of the forms discussed in this chapter (preferably one you have not used before), and think about how you might develop a sermon using that form. You might have a particular biblical text in mind, or you might want to develop a sermon theologically or thematically.

Sketch out the sermon design below.

_____

_____

_____

_____

_____

_____

_____

_____

_____

_____

_____

Notes

1. Richard Ward, *Speaking from the Heart: Preaching with Passion* (Nashville: Abingdon Press, 1992), 77.

2. Cleophus J. LaRue, *I Believe, I'll Testify: The Art of African American Preaching* (Louisville, KY: Westminster John Knox Press, 2011), 24.

3. Eugene L. Lowry, *The Homiletical Plot: The Sermon as Narrative Art Form*, expanded ed. (Louisville, KY: Westminster John Knox Press, 2001).

4. David Buttrick, *Homiletic: Moves and Structures* (Minneapolis: Fortress Press, 1987), 23.

5. Ibid., 33.

6. Ibid., 35. Commentary in italics has been added by the authors.

7. Choan-Seng Song, "Preaching as Shaping Experience in a World of Conflict," in *Preaching as Shaping Experience in a World of Conflict*, ed. Prof. Dr. Albrecht Grözinger and Rev. Dr. Kang Ho Soon (Utrecht: Societas Homiletica, 2005), 29–30.

8. For a fine summation of thirty-four forms with illustrative sermons by a range of distinguished preachers, see Ronald J. Allen, ed., *Patterns of Preaching: A Sermon Sampler* (St. Louis, MO: Chalice Press, 1998).

9. Edmund A. Steimle, Morris J. Niedenthal, and Charles L. Rice, *Preaching the Story* (Minneapolis: Fortress Press, 1980).

10. Edmund A. Steimle, "The Eye of the Storm," in *Preaching the Story*, 121-25. This sermon was preached on Christmas Eve in the 1970s.

11. Prathia Hall, "Between the Wilderness and a Cliff," in *Preaching with Sacred Fire: An Anthology of African American Sermons, 1750 to the Present*, ed. Martha Simmons and Frank A. Thomas (New York: W.W. Norton & Co., 2010), 689–93.

12. Ibid., 690.

13. Ibid., 693.

14. Susan Sparks, "The Mulch Pile," a sermon preached on the Day 1 Radio program, August 2, 2010. See http://day1.org/2242-the_mulch_pile for a transcript of the sermon.

15. Ibid.

16. Ibid.

17. Mary Lin Hudson, "I Dream a World," in *Saved from Silence: Finding Women's Voice in Preaching*, by Mary Lin Hudson and Mary Donovan Turner (St. Louis, MO: Chalice Press, 1999), 117–19. The biblical texts on which the sermon was based are Isaiah 11:1–9; Romans 8:18–25; and Hebrews 11:1–3, 8–16, 12:1–2.

18. Hudson, "I Dream a World," 117–18.

19. Ibid., 118.

20. Ibid., 119.

21. Ibid., 119.

22. Ibid., 120.

23. Harry Emerson Fosdick, "Shall the Fundamentalists Win?" in *A Chorus of Witnesses*, 243–55. The sermon was preached at New York City's First Presbyterian Church in May 1922.

24. Ibid., 252.

25. Ibid., 252.

26. Ibid., 254.

27. Ibid., 255.

28. Samuel D. Proctor, *The Certain Sound of the Trumpet: Crafting a Sermon of Authority* (Valley Forge, PA: Judson Press, 1994).

29. Martin Luther King Jr., "How Should a Christian View Communism?," in *Strength to Love* (Minneapolis: Fortress Press, 1981), 97–106. This sermon was preached during the height of the Cold War and the McCarthy era in American politics.

30. Ibid., 97.

31. Ibid., 98.

32. Ibid., 98.

33. Ibid., 99.

34. Ibid., 100.

35. Ibid., 100–102.

36. Ibid., 103.

37. Ibid., 103–4.

THEOLOGY AND PREACHING

Thus far in this workbook we have looked at important methods for Bible study, for exegeting congregations, and for sermon structuring. In this chapter, we will focus on the core theological convictions that are at the heart of our faith and why we preach them. If we become experts in how to preach, but the theological content of our preaching—the *why* of our preaching—becomes vague or confused or trivialized, then all the methods we have learned will not add up to a hill of beans. Eleazar S. Fernandez reminds us that "there is always the temptation to forget that preaching is first and foremost a theological act, perhaps more so among persons who are strongly committed to preach the gospel as it relates to social issues. Thus, the reminder that preaching is a theological act is relevant and urgent."[1] First, we will talk about why theology matters for preaching. Then each of us is going to share one central theological conviction that it is important for us to preach. Our goal here is not to dictate to you what theological convictions you should preach, for we all have different perspectives on faith and are in different places in our journeys of faith. Rather, we will share one of our core theological convictions in the hopes that it might awaken within you what your own core convictions are.

Post-It Notes of the Human Heart

I, Tom, consider Post-it notes one of the great inventions of the twentieth century. I am referring to those small squares of paper that have a tiny bit of sticky substance along the top that lets you stick them to your refrigerator or in a book or on top of your computer and yet easily remove them. They are ideal for writing things that you are apt to forget. For example:

"Bring home fresh tarragon for tarragon chicken tonight."

"Don't forget dental appointment at 2:30 today."

I find that Post-it notes help me keep the chaos monster at bay. Of course, sometimes I forget to write myself a Post-it note, and I arrive home without the tarragon for the tarragon chicken. When that happens, it is easy enough to make a substitute. Instead of tarragon chicken, it will be garlic chicken tonight.

But there are more important things to remember, things that, if forgotten, have no substitute, things like your child's birthday or your anniversary. There is a hierarchy of things to be remembered. Tarragon is near the bottom. Anniversaries and birthdays are much higher up. But even they are not the most essential things of all to remember. There are certain realities, principles, affirmations, convictions that I call elemental theological truths that we human beings are constantly forgetting, and there is nothing we can substitute for them. These truths lie at the heart and core of the relationship between ourselves and God. When we forget them, our personal life, our relationships, our communities, and the creation that God has entrusted to our care all suffer terribly.

I call these theological truths "elemental" because they are like the physical elements of the material world. They are as essential for living a faithful, abundant life as carbon, oxygen, and hydrogen are to the material world. If it were possible to put up Post-it notes in the human heart, these elemental theological truths are the reminders that I would affix there. Tragically, they keep getting buried beneath all the stuff the human heart accumulates, and so it falls to us preachers to keep reminding ourselves and our listeners of the elemental theological truths that are essential to a faithful life.

Samuel D. Proctor models what it means for preachers to be clear about their elemental theological truths when he lists four propositions that undergird all of his sermons:

> First, basic to the Christian belief system is the understanding of God as absolute, wholly "other," yet present, participating, and aware of the details of all creation, history, and human endeavor, and who can and does intervene on our behalf in the affairs of the world.

> Second, it is also basic to our faith that human nature can be renewed; we can be born again and become new creatures.

> Third, is the conviction that, dismal and remote as it may seem at the moment, the human family can become a genuine community.

> Fourth, also basic is the belief that our earthbound condition, our mundaneness, is given meaning and purpose by the dimension of eternity that is the ever-present potential in our midst. Immortality begins now; eternity flows in the midst of time.[2]

Why Theology Matters for Preaching

In his homiletical textbook *Preaching*, Fred Craddock has a wonderful section on why theology matters for preaching. He writes that

> theology prompts preaching to treat subjects of importance and avoid trivia. How easily sermons seem to err, not on the issue of truth but on the question as to whether what is said really matters. When preparing sermons, if preachers would write "So what?" at the top of the page, many little promotional talks or clever word games on "Salt Shakers and Light Bulbs" would quietly slip off the desk and hide in the wastebasket.
>
> Theology urges upon the pulpit a much larger agenda: creation, evil, grace, covenant, forgiveness, judgment, suffering, care of the earth and all God's creatures, justice, love, and the reconciliation of the world to God. It is not out of order for theology to ask of preaching, What ultimate vision is held before us? Are there words, deeds, and relationships by which we can move toward that vision? How does God look upon us in our stumbling and failure to embrace that vision? It is almost impossible for a sermon on a matter of major importance to the listeners to be totally uninteresting and without impact. But small topics are like pennies; even when polished to a high gloss, they are still pennies.[3]

There is also a confessional quality to preaching on significant theological themes that cannot be underestimated here. I, Nora, remember some years ago reading an article in which a preacher told about how, when he was leaving a parish he had served for many years, he decided that for his last Sunday there he would preach on the topic "What Jesus Means to Me." He preached a highly confessional sermon in which he talked about matters that lie at the heart of the Christian faith and why they were so very important to him in the living of his own life.

He recounted that at the end of the service he stood at the door greeting people and noticed that one of the women who was a member of his congregation stood on the sidelines with tears in her eyes, waiting to speak to him. He falsely assumed she was weeping because she was emotional over his departure. But when the line finally died down and she approached him, this is what she said to him: "What took you so long? Why did you wait until your very last Sunday here to tell us why it all matters so much to you?"

We preachers preach not only in order to share great themes of the faith with our hearers and to keep preaching focused on that which is at the core of the faith. We preach in this way also in order to give testimony to the beliefs that are within us—the beliefs on which we would stake our very lives.

Preaching as Remembering

One of the chief functions of preaching, then, is to remind people of constantly forgotten truth that is essential to their spiritual health, as essential to living an abundant life as air and water. But this act of remembering is not just essential for the congregation. It is equally essential for the ministry of preaching, for it involves being attentive to the core convictions that motivate our preaching. Without such core convictions, preaching can become little more than a weekly chore, something I have to do as a preacher.

What do you hold to be elemental truth in the depths of your being?

In what do you believe so passionately that you want to tell the world?

Choan-Seng Song reminds us that we do not answer these questions in a vacuum.

Instead, our convictions and the way we express them need to engage the most pressing issues of our era:

> The question facing Christian preaching today, whether in Asia or in the West, is this: what is the gospel, the good news, that the Christian church should do its utmost to deliver in a world of conflict, a world torn by conflict of many kinds—racial, sexual, social, political, military, economic, and yes, religious? The answer is compassionate preaching! Preaching with no deep compassion, preaching short of empathetic love, especially towards those who do not share the Christian faith, no matter how true to the tradition and how passionate in its appeal, does not carry much conviction with people who have to bear the brunt of conflicts not of their own making. . . . God's compassion is robust passion with those who suffer. It is the willingness to side with the victims of injustice. It is the spiritual capacity to embrace those who are at the other end of the conflict, making genuine efforts to see things from their perspective.[4]

Our Core Convictions

We are each going to identify one core conviction that vitalizes our preaching.

Although it sometimes figures prominently in this or that sermon, it is not a constant theme in all of our preaching. Rather, it is an elemental theological truth that keeps stirring the fire in our hearts, keeps us returning again and again to the Word of God, to the risen Christ, to the living Spirit, and to the task of preaching with renewed inspiration. Of course, we each have more than one conviction. But we share these with you in order to stir you to identify a core conviction that makes you want to preach and that can sustain your preaching for the long haul.

Tom's Core Conviction

My core conviction comes from Psalm 100. I quote it the way my early childhood pastor frequently spoke it in worship, because that is the way it became imprinted on my heart: "It is the Lord who has made us and not we ourselves." That our life and being do not originate in anything we ever did is an elemental theological truth that we keep forgetting. Artificial environments and virtual reality continually obscure this basic fact. The result is arrogance that leads to absolutism in the realm of politics and environmental destruction in the realm of nature. When we know with all our heart and mind that "it is the Lord who has made us and not we ourselves," then we realize our very existence is a gift, and we respond with gratitude and humility to the One who is the source of all being. Our moral life is reframed by our responsibility to the Creator who has granted us the wonder of existence as a feeling, thinking, relating creature.

Nora's Core Conviction

My core conviction comes from that familiar Easter refrain that we used to shout out every Easter Sunday morning in the church where I served in New York City. The pastor would begin worship by proclaiming, "Christ is risen!" and all the people would loudly respond, "Christ is risen indeed!"

In his 2011 Lyman Beecher lectures at Yale Divinity School, biblical scholar Brian Blount reminded us of how critical that affirmation is to what we as Christians believe.[5] In the midst of a death-dealing culture, a culture in which people around us are sometimes the "living dead" as we go about the world giving our allegiances to things that lead to death and not life, we Christians bring a word of enormous hope: namely, that death will not have the last word in our world, but that God—the same God who miraculously raised Christ from death to life—is still at work in our world bringing hope out of despair, joy out of sorrow, and yes, life out of death.

Existentially, I know this to be true in my own life, because when I was brought face to face with my own mortality during a battle with cancer a number of years ago, it was to this promise at the core of our faith that I clung. I had two mantras that saw me through those days when I felt like I was walking in the valley of the shadow of death: the first was "the sun still rises"—which is both creation-based and rooted in resurrection hope. As I would sit on my sun porch in the early morning hours, wrapped in a quilt and waiting for dawn to break, I never ceased to be grateful for the rising of the sun and the promise of hope it brought to each new day. If God was still in control, if resurrection—and not death—had the last word, then there was hope to face another grueling day of tests and treatments and illness.

The second mantra that I clung to during that time—a mantra that followed from the first (I now see in retrospect)—was that wonderful quotation of the mystic Julian of Norwich: "All shall be well and all shall be well and all manner of things shall be well." If Christ is indeed risen, if the sun still rises, then at the core of my being I can rest in the certain hope that indeed "all shall be well, and all shall be well, and all manner of things shall be well." And I can trust that reality, not only for my own individual life, but also for the life of this entire broken and hurting and diseased world.

EXERCISE: THEOLOGY AND PREACHING

1. Identify one core conviction that makes you want to preach and that can sustain your preaching.

   _____

   What are the challenges of preaching it in ways that sound fresh and new and can engage people now?

   _____

   _____

   _____

2. Discuss your answers to these questions in small groups, and with the group as a whole.

   _____

   _____

Notes

1. Eleazar S. Fernandez, "A Filipino Perspective: 'Unfinished Dream' in the Land of Promise," in *Preaching Justice: Ethnic and Cultural Perspectives*, ed. Christine Marie Smith (Cleveland, OH: United Church Press, 1998), 63.

2. Cited in O. C. Edwards Jr., *A History of Preaching* (Nashville: Abingdon Press, 2004), 721. The original reference is from Samuel D. Proctor, *How Shall They Hear? Effective Preaching for Vital Christian Faith* (Valley Forge, PA: Judson Press, 1992), 16–17.

3. Fred B. Craddock, *Preaching* (Nashville: Abingdon Press, 1985), 49.

4. Choan-Seng Song, "Preaching as Shaping Experience in a World of Conflict," in *Preaching as Shaping Experience in a World of Conflict*, ed. Prof. Dr. Albrecht Grözinger and Rev. Dr. Kang Ho Soon (Utrecht: Societas Homiletica, 2005), 28.

5. Brian K. Blount, Lyman Beecher Lectures at Yale Divinity School, October 2011. The overall theme of Blount's lectures was "Invasion of the Dead: Preaching Resurrection Through the Lens of Apocalyptic Eschatology."

MAKING THEOLOGY INCARNATE FOR PREACHING

Preachers are often called upon to start with large abstract theological concepts such as sin, salvation, or grace, and then to unpack them in ways that allow people to see or experience them in relation to their own lives. Frankly, this making of theology "incarnate" through our words is one of the hardest challenges of preaching. One of the greatest temptations ministers will face is either using these words and concepts in sermons without defining them at all—an especially problematic practice in a day when so many of the people sitting in our pews did not grow up attending church or being schooled in the faith—or, alternatively, falling prey to cliché.

The author Nora Gallagher illustrates the dangers involved in both temptations in an article she wrote for the Yale Divinity School journal *Reflections*.[1] Gallagher begins her article by telling a story of visiting an Episcopal church in New York City one Good Friday and finding, in the middle of the service, that she was bored. She writes, "I was bored the way I am when I listen to someone telling me nothing new or when someone gives me prepackaged, generic phrases in place of authentic feeling and experience. I was bored the way I was in fifth grade when the teacher went through a lesson I had already studied and understood."[2]

A few months later, Gallagher was teaching a week-long class to a group of divinity school graduates (mostly clergy) on writing:

> As the class began, my Good Friday experience was still on my mind. On the second day, we "workshopped" a manuscript by a woman who serves a parish on the Eastern Seaboard, a newsletter article about "celebrations." I had been worried about this manuscript from the moment I read it. The word "blessing" was used a number of times without a full sense of what was meant by it. The Bible and the *Book of Common Prayer* were quoted and so was the Oxford English Dictionary. I felt as if the writer were circling a subject that lay off to the side. It did not add up. I was bored by it.
>
> In the class, I asked the author if there was anything she wished to say to us before we dove in.
>
> "Yes," she replied. "The whole thing is a lie."
>
> A collective gasp went up.
>
> "It's a lie," she said. "I don't really like celebrations. Or at least not all of them. I am not sure they are 'blessings.' I don't even know what 'blessing' means. I was asked to write this the day before it was due for the church newsletter and I wrote it as if I were asleep, read it over, hated it, and sent it in."
>
> We burst into applause.
>
> The week went on that way; student after student found the places in their manuscripts where either a lie was told or the truth was obscured. On the very last day, I asked a minister from Virginia exactly what she meant by the phrase in her sermon about "being cleansed by the blood of Jesus," and after some thought, she replied, "I don't know."

I realized that week that my twenty-one students, as bright and lively and passionate about their work as you could find in ministry, were victimized by the same thing that so oppressed me in that church on Good Friday: the deadening force of words that are no longer enfleshed or carry meaning. And, although I can't be sure this was the case in that church on that Friday, I will bet that there, too, was the fear of telling the truth about one's experience. Add to that, inside-the-beltway lingo, cheery optimism, unearned hope (those hasty flourishes of hope tacked onto the end of a sermon or article without letting the material itself lead us there). *Getting things right.* These are pitfalls of religious writing and they are pitfalls of church practice.[3]

Toward the end of her article, Gallagher adds these telling lines: "I think we were trapped in that Good Friday service and in many of our church services and in our writing about faith, behind the 'screen of clichés.' *The connections between words and what they signify has been broken. The first human power—the power to name—is failing.*"[4]

The fact of the matter is that we preachers face a linguistic quandary. Our tradition passes on to us many words that no longer have great currency in everyday speech, but we cannot afford to abandon them because they express essential theological truth that our culture either neglects or actively rejects.[5] For example, in a culture that stresses feeling good about oneself, "sin" seems an antiquated yet disturbing word that many would like to avoid. But if we give up "sin," we give up an important insight about the fragmented lives and distorted values that are very much with us and are the deadly realities that Christ engages and overcomes. If we lose the use of the word "sin," we lose as well the use of "salvation." If there is no sin, there is no need to be saved from it. Giving up these words means our preaching will work at a superficial level, instead of addressing, as the gospel does, the profound brokenness of human existence and the astounding news of God's transforming grace in Christ.

The burden on the preacher, then, is to find ways to bring the great words of faith alive so that people grasp the redeeming truth to which they point.

This process often requires us to find connecting points between church doctrine and contemporary lived experience. Richard Thulin observes, "The preacher who struggles to establish such a relationship is functioning as a theologian. She or he is working to make sense of inherited truth, to find reciprocal access between the faith and experienced human life. Theological thinking involves more than repeating crystallized statements of doctrine. It involves sensing the human experience out of which doctrine arises and for which doctrine should serve as a catalyst."[6]

Instead of giving up our theological treasures, we press our imaginations into service to ask how these truths are embodied, how they are incarnate in this world, how we smell and see and hear and feel and taste them in this world. Here is an exercise that invites you to engage in the art of honest and creative theological naming, an art essential for effective preaching.

EXERCISE: SENSORY DESCRIPTIONS OF THEOLOGICAL CONCEPTS

1. Take one of the following five theological terms, and describe it in relation to all five of the senses.

Sin
Salvation
Grace
Holiness
Reign of God

_____ looks like . . .

_____ tastes like . . .

_____ smells like . . .

_____ feels like (bodily weight) . . .

_____ sounds like . . .

2. Choose any one of the five statements you have written, and elaborate on it for three to four sentences.

_____

_____

_____

_____

_____

For Further Reflection

1. Discuss your answers to the exercise questions in small groups of three or four.

2. If in a classroom setting, have several volunteers read the paragraphs they have written aloud to the entire class.

Notes

1. Nora Gallagher, "Breaking through the Screen of Cliché," *Reflections* 96, No. 2 (Fall 2009): 57–59.

2. Ibid., 58.

3. Ibid. Italics added by the author.

4. Ibid., 59. Italics added by Gallagher to indicate her use of material from the essay "The Production of the World" by John Berger, whose phrase "screen of clichés" likewise inspired her title.

5. I, Tom, am indebted here to Gene E. Bartlett, one of my former homiletics teachers who was a master at bringing alive the key terms of Christian faith. See his Lyman Beecher lectures, published as *The Audacity of Preaching: The Lyman Beecher Lectures Yale Divinity School 1961* (New York: Harper & Brothers, 1962).

6. Richard L. Thulin, *The "I" of the Sermon* (Eugene, OR: Wipf and Stock Publishers, 2000), 15.

IDENTIFYING CONGREGATIONAL RESISTANCES TO PREACHING

One of the major challenges facing the preacher is identifying and addressing the resistances people bring to a sermon and its reception. We are dealing here with the realm of theological anthropology: trying to understand human beings more deeply and why they put up the walls they sometimes do when hearing sermons. While some of the resistances congregants bring to worship are beyond our control—for example, the various life and church experiences that have shaped the ways in which parishioners hear our words—there are often things we preachers can do to help break through some resistances and speak a word that lodges itself in the human heart.

In her book *Transforming the Stone*, Lutheran pastor and homiletician Barbara Lundblad claims that frequently what is at the heart of people's resistance to sermons is fear. Sermons are often asking people to change, and people fear change. Consequently, they respond not with an open embrace of the message we are bringing, but with defensiveness and resistance to it:

As we look around the landscape of our country and the larger world, we need to acknowledge that many, including ourselves, are scrambling to secure a place, to shore up the shifting sands:

- *Shore up the borders!* Build a barrier to keep out immigrants (at least, those we don't want).

- *Shore up the streets!* Remove the homeless from our neighborhoods. Make us safer by legalizing the death penalty.

- *Shore up the family!* Pass the "Defense of Marriage Act" to protect traditional values.

- *Shore up the church!* Return to tradition. Silence the voice of feminists. Get back to the Bible.

If we listen carefully to the words and the emotions behind the words, we hear a great deal of fear. Beneath the appeals to scripture and creeds, the voices often sound like the angriest callers to radio talk shows. Personal opinions and deep feelings are equated with what God said. With so many changes swirling around in the culture, the church may seem like the last familiar foundation that we can hold on to.[1]

Unless we name and address the fears people have in our preaching, claims Lundblad, people may not be able to move through resistance to embrace change.

Taking People's Resistance Seriously

James Dittes was a pastoral theologian who wrote at length about why people say "No" to a minister's leadership. Dittes built on a central insight from counseling: therapists often sense they are getting closest to what really matters to an individual when the person begins to resist them. Likewise, the "No" from congregants may indicate the minister is dealing with something that is of crucial importance to them:

> No is a groan. . . . No is hardly more articulate than ouch and often means much the same thing: something (or perhaps everything) hurts or threatens, and I must reflexively back away. No, like ouch, usually signals pain and fear . . . the only way to minister to it is through it. The minister enters into the experience of the groaning no, sharing it as partner, rather than fighting it as the adversary . . . The minister tries to feel what it is like to be this person coming close but turning away.[2]

While Dittes was writing about ministerial leadership in general, Milton Crum has developed a homiletical method for dealing with resistance to the gospel in sermons. Included is an analysis of the ineffective strategies that preachers sometimes use: "Can you imagine being persuaded through being scolded by a TV commercial for not buying its product? The point is that our behavior is based on our perceptions; therefore, to change voluntary behavior, perception must be changed."[3]

Instead of moralizing and scolding, Crum asks, "What is the complication [in my life] that prevents my doing that which I know I should? In what beliefs and perceptions is the symptomatic behavior rooted?"[4] Crum says preachers should ask this question of themselves in order to "map" the human resistance to the gospel that is alive in the preacher as well as the congregation. As part of their sermon preparation, preachers ask what would open their own hearts to God's challenging word. What would overcome their resistance? Preachers draw upon their own humanity to understand the humanity of their congregants. Instead of scolding, they enter the depths of the human heart to understand its resistance, as well as its hunger for the word of God.

In the exercise that follows, we ask you to reflect on three different biblical passages, asking, what good reasons might we and others have for resisting the message this text brings? And, what might the preacher do in a sermon on these texts to help the congregation move from resistance to change?

EXERCISE: IDENTIFYING RESISTANCES TO PREACHING

Choose one of the following biblical passages and read it aloud, either on your own or in a small group. If you are in a classroom setting, it would be helpful to have all three passages discussed by different small groups.

1. Micah 6:6–8

"With what shall I come before
 the LORD,
 and bow myself before God on high?
Shall I come before him with
 burnt offerings,
 with calves a year old?
Will the LORD be pleased with
 thousands of rams,
 with ten thousands of rivers of oil?
Shall I give my firstborn for my
 transgression,
 the fruit of my body for the sin of my soul?"
He has told you, O mortal, what
 is good;
 and what does the LORD
 require of you
but to do justice, and to love
 kindness,
 and to walk humbly with your God?

2. John 5:1–9

After this there was a festival of the Jews, and Jesus went up to Jerusalem. Now in Jerusalem by the Sheep Gate there is a pool, called in Hebrew Beth-zatha, which has five porticoes. In these lay many invalids—blind, lame, and paralyzed. One man was there who had been ill for thirty-eight years. When Jesus saw him lying there and knew that he had been there a long time, he said to him, "Do you want to be made well?" The sick man answered him, "Sir, I have no one to put me into the pool when the water is stirred up; and while I am making my way, someone else steps down ahead of me." Jesus said to him, "Stand up, take your mat and walk." At once the man was made well, and he took up his mat and began to walk.

3. Ephesians 4:1–6

I therefore, the prisoner in the Lord, beg you to lead a life worthy of the calling to which you have been called, with all humility and gentleness, with patience, bearing with one another in love, making every effort to maintain the unity of the Spirit in the bond of peace. There is one body and one Spirit, just as you were called to the one hope of your calling, one Lord, one faith, one baptism, one God and Father of all, who is above all and through all and in all.

Write your answers to the following questions:

1. What are the resistances you personally might have to hearing and embracing the message of this passage?

_____

_____

2. What are resistances you either have encountered in others, or can imagine others having to this message?

_____

_____

3. What would help you overcome your resistance and embrace the message? Do you need reassurance? Do you need information? Do you need the perspective of another worldview? Do you need some new dream or vision? Other?

_____

_____

4. What specific strategies might you use in a sermon on this text to address and overcome resistances on the part of your hearers?

_____

_____

Discuss your answers in small groups, and then in the group as a whole.

For Further Reflection

What did you find more difficult: naming the resistances, or coming up with strategies to address them? Why do you think this was so?

Notes

1. Barbara K. Lundblad, *Transforming the Stone: Preaching through Resistance to Change* (Nashville: Abingdon Press, 2001), 15.

2. James E. Dittes, *When the People Say No: Conflict and the Call to Ministry* (New York: Harper & Row, Publishers, 1979), 28.

3. Milton Crum Jr., *Manual on Preaching* (Valley Forge, PA: Judson Press, 1977), 37.

4. Ibid., 29.

ADDRESSING CONGREGATIONAL RESISTANCES THROUGH PREACHING

As you may have discovered in undertaking the exercise at the end of the previous chapter, it is often far easier to name the resistances congregations have to a sermon than it is to identify strategies for addressing and overcoming them. In this chapter, we will discuss eight strategies that can be useful in helping the preacher move listeners beyond resistance to a willingness to consider and even be changed by a challenging biblical sermon.

Before we do so, however, it is important to state clearly what we are *not* trying to do here, as well as what we are aiming for. We are *not* trying to make the difficult words of Scripture more palatable for people. We are *not* trying to water down the gospel so that its message is less offensive. We are *not* trying to blunt the Bible's prophetic witness. Rather, what we *are* aiming for is a style and mode of communication that helps people set aside their initial resistances to what Scripture may say to them, and open themselves to a fresh hearing of it. In the process, we are trying to rid our own sermons of any "false stumbling blocks"—that is, unintentional blocks that we as preachers are putting in the way of our hearers—that prohibit their giving our messages a fair hearing.[1]

Eight Strategies for Addressing Congregational Resistances

1. Stand with the people under the word of God, rather than opposite the people armed with the word of God.

Biblical scholar Walter Brueggemann[2] once compared the dynamic of communication in preaching with that of family systems theory. In each act of proclamation, said Brueggemann, there are three actors: the preacher, the biblical text, and the congregation. All too often, what happens in preaching is that the preacher and the biblical text team up against (that is, "triangle" against) the congregation in the sermon. (See first triangle on page 98.) Consequently, the people are understandably resistant and even hostile to hearing what the sermon has to say. They are left without a leg to stand on! Far better, Brueggemann argued, if both preacher and congregation stand *under* the word of God that offends both.[3] (See second triangle on page 98.)

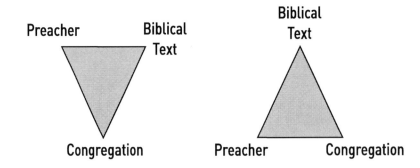

When preachers stand with the people under the word of God, rather than opposite the people armed with the word of God, the whole tone of the sermon shifts. The preacher no longer stands in an accusatory role, bringing a word of judgment from God upon a recalcitrant people. Rather, the preacher places himself or herself on the same level as the people as "we" wrestle together with God's offensive word that judges us all.

Biblical scholar Brian Blount once preached a sermon to graduating seniors at Princeton Theological Seminary in which he used this strategy very effectively. The sermon, entitled "Stay Close," is based on the story in Mark 9:14–29 in which Jesus heals a demon-possessed boy and then challenges the disciples to pray hard so that they, too, can cast out demons in Jesus' name. This excerpt comes near the sermon's end:

> But before I close I must come clean myself. You know, when I first heard about this invitation [to preach to you graduates], my first inclination was to turn it down. Not because I'm not honored that you would ask me to preach at such an important occasion (which I am), but because I was a little afraid. Not of preaching, but of preaching in this academic context. I never preached in this chapel while I was a student, and when I returned, I honestly intended not to preach here as a professor. When I was a student it was because it always felt more like an academic exercise than a spiritual one because I felt, even then, that I was being graded. Now it's because I remember how my sermons in my community in Virginia sometimes got me in trouble, and junior professors already have all the trouble they can handle just by being junior professors. I worry about that kind of stuff all the time, it seems now. About how people perceive me. About whether I'm doing too much. Saying too much. About how far I have the resources to push myself beyond the confines of this sheltered seminary existence to work where I ought to be working in the world around it. . . .
>
> Believe me, there will come a time when you start to worry in the same way. Worry about offending parishioners, threatening the budget, offending powerful people on the session, in the presbytery, on the deacons' board, in the bishop's office, in the mayor's office, on the school board, on the chamber of commerce, in the PTS community, and you start to think, you know, "I've got a family. I want to have friends. I want people to like me. I want to keep my job or secure it for a long time." So you start to think, "Maybe I ought to do Christianity, do faith the way Brian Blount plays basketball, without risk, without doing anything that might push me to the point of no return." I'm here tonight, though, because I want to tell you, and remind myself, if that's what you've graduated to do, then maybe your presbytery can use you, maybe your bishop can use you, maybe your church can use you.
>
> But I'm not so sure God can use you.
>
> Appears to me, by then you're pretty much all used up. God needs soldiers, not used-up followers. God needs players who can give God twenty points every night. That's what finally came to me as I meditated on the decision to worship with you this evening. I thought about my father struggling and believing. I thought about those slaves singing and believing. In cotton fields, in cornfields, in tobacco fields, in fields of misery and hopelessness, and yet they sang the Lord's song in a foreign land. They stayed close to God, and that gave them faith, and the faith gave them power.[4]

2. Re-contextualize the passage.

I (Tom) recall a recent occasion when I was asked to preach on the Good Samaritan (Luke 10:25–37). Like many preachers, I could not count the number of times this had been a text for a sermon I had heard or delivered myself. My initial thought was "Do I have anything more to say about the Good Samaritan than what I have heard and said through all these years?" I the preacher was resisting the passage I was asked to preach on, and I have spoken with many church members who have a similar resistance. Having sat through so many sermons on the parable, they assume they know what it is about. They suffer from the "I've-heard-it-all-before" syndrome.

One of the factors that reinforces the resistance bred of familiarity is that people read biblical passages as isolated stories. The result is that the preacher may fail to consider how the story fits into the larger narrative or logical structure of the biblical book from which it is drawn, and it is that greater, overarching view that can sometimes loosen resistance and open us to insights we never had before. In this case, I undertook a word study on the word "Samaritan," looking up every time Luke uses the term in Luke/Acts. I made astonishing discoveries.

In Luke 9, the disciples ask Jesus if he wants them to call down fire on the Samaritans because they had refused him hospitality. Jesus rebukes the disciples, but in the next chapter he effectively makes a much more dramatic response to their request. He tells a story in which the good guy is a Samaritan, a member of the very group that recently rejected him and the disciples wanted to firebomb! Imagine how that must have grated on the disciples.

But Luke does not end his references to the Samaritans with Jesus' famous parable. Later, in Acts 8, Luke recounts how Peter and John proclaimed "the good news to many villages of the Samaritans" (Acts 8:25). The larger narrative structure of Luke/Acts reveals that it is not just the wounded victim on the road to Jericho who is healed (Luke 10:29–35). By featuring the kindness of a Samaritan in his parable, Jesus was healing the alienation between the Jews and the Samaritans. Refusing to give in to the prejudice and animosity between these groups, Jesus ends up transforming the disciples so they become messengers of the gospel to the group they once wanted to destroy. The parable *set in its full biblical context* is not only about doing individual acts of kindness: it is about the healing of the rifts and hatred that separate the human race. This insight, however, is available only by moving outside the parable to consider how it functions in the larger narrative of Luke/Acts. When I realized this previously hidden dimension to the story, my resistance to preaching on the text dissolved, and many listeners were grateful because they had never thought of the story from that angle before.

Contextualizing a biblical passage is not limited to placing a passage in the greater framework of the canon. We can also contextualize a passage by varying the social and cultural milieu from which we view it. This can be particularly effective when one is going to preach on issues of social justice and poverty among those who are more privileged. In an insecure world, these issues understandably can touch off resistance in the forms of self-defensiveness or guilt. Neither of these will empower people to seek change or to minister to a wounded world, and yet the gospel clearly calls us to work for justice and compassion.

I have never forgotten a strategy James Forbes used in preaching on these issues many years ago. He began by reading the beatitudes (Matthew 5:1–12), and then asked us, a privileged middle-class congregation, to review what thoughts, feelings, and images had arisen in us as he was reading. Forbes was silent for a moment, allowing us time to review our response to the familiar and beloved words. Then he told us about a recent trip to a barrio in South America, a slum that was wretchedly impoverished. He described the garbage; the look and stench of it;

the rats; the shelters of plywood, cardboard, and rusting corrugated steel; children begging or playing a game of kick-the-can down the alley; men lying drunk in the streets or sitting on stairs with gaunt, empty faces; women with desperate-looking eyes who tended crying babies; and, amidst all this, a small rectangular building with a bare table adorned with a simple cross at one end and crates and some chairs for people to sit on and a dirt floor and a small band playing some lively music to which people were singing and swaying and moving their uplifted hands. He invited us into the church and asked us to imagine the music stopping and the preacher opening a Bible and reading. At this point, Forbes opened the Bible again and read once more the beatitudes. It was the exact same passage, but placed in this new context, I heard it in ways I never before heard or read it. He had re-contextualized my listening, my understanding, and moved me beyond resistance to an eagerness to hear what he had to say about justice and liberation of those oppressed by crushing poverty.

3. Start with the familiar and comfortable and move toward the unfamiliar to help the congregation stretch toward what is new.

Sometimes it is helpful to think about the trajectory a sermon takes in pressing toward change, and, rather than confronting people head on with the hoped-for modification in belief or behavior, gradually ease into it by first naming practices and beliefs that are more familiar and comfortable.[5]

Once again, we draw for illustration on the ministry of James Forbes because he is a preacher who over the years has worked again and again to find homiletical strategies to engage people in vital issues they might otherwise resist. In this sermon, delivered when he was the senior pastor at Riverside Church in New York City, Forbes models the practice of beginning with the familiar and comfortable, then moving on to what is more disturbing and challenging. Notice also how he embodies Milton Crum's strategy of dealing with his own resistance (chapter 13), sharing it directly in the sermon. This helps Forbes to stand under God's prophetic word along with the congregation rather than above and against them (strategy 1 in this chapter):

> Years ago, when I was still living in North Carolina, someone said to me, "Brother Forbes, do you think the gospel can be preached by someone who is not Pentecostal?" Well, I wasn't sure, for it was the only preaching I had known, but I imagined that it could happen even if I hadn't seen or heard it. Indeed, I found out some time later that it was so.
>
> After I had moved away from my hometown, someone said to me, "Reverend Forbes, have you ever heard the true gospel from a white preacher?" Well, in theory I knew it had to be true, for God doesn't withhold the Spirit from anyone. Though I had my doubts that a white preacher could speak with power, I came to a point in my life where I had to say, "Yes, I've heard it!"
>
> Some time went by, and people began to press upon me the question of the ordination of women. "Could the gospel be preached by a woman even though the holy scriptures bid a woman to keep silence in the church?" I had to ponder this, for it went against what I had known in my own church and there was much resistance from my brother clergy. But I listened to my sisters and before too long I knew the Spirit of God was calling them to preach. Who was I to get in God's way?
>
> Now I thought I had been asked the last question about who might be called to bring me the word of the Lord. But I found out I was wrong. A new question has been posed to me and many of you know what it is. "Can gay men and lesbian women be called to preach the word of God?" Oh, I know what the Bible says and I know what my own uneasiness says and I can see that same uneasiness in some of your faces. But I've been wrong before, and the Spirit has been nudging me to get over my uneasiness. Sometimes we forget Jesus' promise—that the Spirit will lead us into all the truth. Well, that must have meant the disciples didn't know it all then, and maybe we don't know it all now.[6]

4. Honor what people consider sacred and beautiful, and use it as a source of transformative power.

During the late 1960s and early 1970s, the Vietnam War was tearing apart many congregations. Large numbers of pastors preached against the war, and although their sermons were well received by the so-called "doves," the "hawks" and the large number of people who were neither hawk nor dove often protested that the preachers were misusing the pulpit. I have never forgotten the contrast between the ways two different preachers approached the issue on a Christmas Eve when the war was prominently in the news.

One preacher dispensed with the traditional Christmas Eve service, carols, and sermon and showed an anti-war movie, claiming it was the only way he could imagine celebrating the birth of the Prince of Peace in light of the carnage in Vietnam. The doves in his congregation were nearly as furious with him as the hawks and all the others. He had violated one of the most sacred services of the year, and in doing so, lost connection even with his supporters.

The other preacher, equally disturbed by the war, planned the traditional service, carols, and sermon. He began his sermon by telling the birth narrative from the perspective of Joseph. I do not remember the whole sermon, but the opening section is still with me forty-something years later. The preacher, wielding a hammer, struck a nail once and said "Taxes!" then struck the nail again, "Taxes!" then one more hammer blow, "Taxes!" "Caesar Augustus has made a decree that all the world is to be taxed. Mary, who is pregnant, and I have to travel back to my hometown, risking her health and the child she is carrying just so Caesar can raise the funds he needs to support the Roman military industrial complex. . . ." The sermon became a reflection on the birth of Christ in a violent world. The preacher drew on the details of the birth narrative, including the slaughter of the innocent, to make it clear why there was no way he could preach on Christmas Eve and not mention the war: to do so would require ignoring the violence in the biblical story. It would not be faithful to the sacred tradition.

Of course, the sermon did not convert everyone to his position, but it did significantly lower the resistance to addressing the war in church, both in sermons and in parish conversations in the following months. No one could forget those hammer blows and "Taxes!" Even those who disagreed with the preacher's stance agreed that his reading of the sacred tradition was faithful to what was in the biblical text and that it gave theological warrant for his insistence on engaging the issue.

5. Use a congregation's own history as a connecting point to stretch the congregation.

When William Sloane Coffin wanted to announce the establishment of a major new anti-disarmament center at Riverside Church in New York City in 1978 (Coffin was at the time senior pastor of the church), he did three things in his Sunday morning sermon, titled "Warring Madness," that helped connect that initiative with Riverside's past history. First, Coffin preached the sermon on the weekend closest to the one hundredth anniversary of the birth of Harry Emerson Fosdick, Riverside's much beloved founding pastor. Second, Coffin quoted two of Fosdick's most famous sermons—"Shall the Fundamentalists Win?" and "The Unknown Soldier"—in his own sermon. Because "The Unknown Soldier" was the sermon in which Fosdick had first publicly declared himself to be a pacifist, Coffin's quoting of it also reminded the church of its own long history of involvement in peacemaking initiatives. Third, he took the title of the sermon "Warring Madness" from a much cherished hymn text by Fosdick, "God of Grace and God of Glory," which includes the line "Cure thy children's warring madness." And finally, Coffin announced that the church was establishing the fund in Fosdick's honor.[7]

Often, resistances to preaching can be lessened if the preacher can help the congregation see the connections between the new vision that is being offered and the church's own past values and mission involvement.[8]

6. Start with broader church or world history.

I (Tom) do not know who first said it, so I cannot give a reference for the following quotation, but I have heard it in many sermons and church conversations over the years: "The problem with most old-time religion is that it is not old enough." For many people, their old-time religion goes back only as far as their childhood, and their truncated historical vision often results in a truncated understanding of faith and the practices of the church. As a result of this limited perspective, people often resist innovation because "we have never done that before" or "it is not part of our tradition." One effective strategy for addressing this kind of resistance is to preach about the depth and breadth of one's tradition and the church universal.

I think, for example, of a Presbyterian pastor who got tired of hearing his own congregants describing themselves as "the frozen chosen." He preached a sermon filled with revealing stories from the history of the reformed faith that is central to Presbyterian identity. He told about the fervent singing of psalms, introducing some of the original lively musical settings in the body of the sermon and after its conclusion. He drew upon diaries and letters from early Calvinists to show how deeply moved they were in worship services. One of the letters featured a phrase that described the impact of John Calvin's preaching on the congregation: "Grown men wept unabashedly at the clear preaching of the word of God." The preacher used the broader, longer history of the tradition to melt away the concept of "the frozen chosen."

In a similar fashion, I recall a student who preached a sermon in chapel back in the late 1970s, when I was first teaching homiletics. At the time, many denominations were struggling with the ordination of women. Even those who did ordain women found a lot of resistance to the practice, and frequently there was an unwillingness to call a woman as pastor. In her sermon, the student quoted from an address, "Ain't I a Woman?" delivered by Sojourner Truth in 1851 at the Women's Convention in Akron, Ohio. Although in the succeeding decades I have heard the words quoted many times, I will never forget how forceful they were in the context of the struggle for women's ordination:

> Then that little man in black there, he says women can't have as much rights as men, 'cause Christ wasn't a woman! Where did your Christ come from? Where did your Christ come from? From God and a woman! Man had nothing to do with Him.
>
> If the first woman God ever made was strong enough to turn the world upside down all alone, these women together ought to be able to turn it back, and get it right side up again! And now they is asking to do it, the men better let them.[9]

The witness of history came alive in the sermon and inspired the listeners to persist in their efforts to have women ordained.

I think also of a conference on music in worship that I helped lead for pastors in Northern Germany and Denmark. Many people believe ours is the first age of controversy about what music is appropriate for church and the strong resistance that some congregants have to innovation and others have to tradition. But our era is not the first to face this conflict. It goes all the way back to the early church fathers, and it continues in other periods of church song. Searching through the stacks of the library, I found a book that was filled with historical goodies, giving witness to earlier debates about music and worship that the churches of northern Europe had endured, the very region that the conferees served! The introduction to the *Hamburg Melodeyen Gesangbuch* of 1604 disparages the new Italian styles that were spreading into Germany during the early 1600s:

> Wherever instead of fine, serious motets and moving psalms and songs that touch the heart, pieces and songs that come frolicking in with a skip are sung by choir with organ, and played with foreign, Italian lascivious leaps and tick-tacks, or strange fugues, as if one were going to the dance, then not only can no devotion ensue, but a distaste for lovely and magnificent music must thereby be inserted and grafted on to the hearts of those present.[10]

Heinrich Mithobius, a Lutheran pastor at Otterndorf, near Hamburg, answered the critics of the new styles of music in his Christian Psalms, 1665: "Meanwhile at this time of ours [God] fills many excellent composers with his spirit, who have composed the most magnificent musical art pieces, and proved therein their high understanding and art in music."[11]

When the congregation of pastors heard these quotations, their faces broke into smiles. There was comfort and reassurance in knowing that their ancestors in the faith who had once ministered in the regions they now serve had dealt with the same struggles centuries earlier. The historical knowledge provided in the sermon aided them in overcoming their own resistance to facing the issue.

Another way I phrase this strategy is "Draw upon the cloud of witnesses." It is the same strategy used by the author of the Book of Hebrews, who, after naming one hero of the faith after another, refers to how we are "surrounded by so great a cloud of witnesses" and exhorts us to "run with perseverance the race that is set before us" (Hebrews 12:1). A broad and deep understanding of tradition is a major homiletical resource for loosening the resistance that results from a constricted knowledge of the church's history.

7. Use personal stories or testimonies to help humanize larger social or theological issues.

While congregations may sometimes grow resistant when the preacher announces that she is preaching on a large social issue such as war or immigration reform or domestic violence, one way to counter those resistances is to "personalize" the issue through the use of story or testimony. The story may be the preacher's own, or it may be that of someone else who is well acquainted with the issue. But the goals are the same: namely, to help the hearers connect more viscerally with the issue at hand by personalizing it, and to help the congregation see more clearly why their own response to the issue matters.

I (Nora) once attended a worship service in which the preacher was trying to help bolster congregational involvement with and support for a community program that assisted former prisoners with their transitions back into society. Rather than talking extensively herself about the program and its purposes and needs, this pastor wisely invited someone who had been through the program and benefitted from it to give testimony—in the midst of the sermon—to the difference the program had made in her life. The congregation was deeply moved by this woman's testimony and was helped to recognize, in a more visceral way, the difference the program was actually making in the lives of real human beings.[12]

In a sermon she preached on domestic violence, Anna Marie Hunter courageously used her own past personal experience with domestic violence both to convict her congregation regarding the church's past sins in not supporting women who are the victims of such violence, and to spur them to become "manna in the wilderness"[13]—providing personal support and public advocacy— for women who are currently in such situations. Early in her sermon, she writes,

I was in an abusive marriage for four years. I stayed because I had made a vow before God; I had been taught to forgive seven times seventy; I had been told to turn the other cheek; I had learned to forgive and forget. I stayed because of some of my best qualities: I am loyal, hard-working, determined, and persistent. I do not easily break commitments. I take responsibility for making my relationships work. When you are a victim of domestic violence, even your own best qualities will be used as weapons against you.[14]

Later, Hunter gives testimony to the church's failure of her at her time of deepest need:

Shortly after I left my abusive marriage, my priest called me in to talk to him. I had not told him what was going on because no one in my church had ever talked about domestic violence, so I assumed that I was the first one this had ever happened to. I gladly went in to talk to the priest because I knew that I needed the support of my religious community.

It turned out that my husband had called the priest and "filled him in" on the situation. So the priest started our meeting by asking me why I had abandoned my marriage. Already upset at the word "abandoned," I stammered out that when I tried to be myself in this marriage, my partner would get violent. That was the opening the priest needed. "All you people in the younger generation think about is me, me, me," he shouted at me. "You are always abandoning your commitments to other people in order to be yourself or find yourself." He then told me that my husband had had a religious conversion and was in the chapel on his knees at that very moment, praying for me to come back. "Now it's your turn to forgive and forget."[15]

And finally, toward her sermon's end, Hunter gives testimony to the power of the gospel to liberate and heal, and to a revised theology that has arisen out of this life experience:

It has been sixteen years since I left my abuser. I have gone to seminary and become a pastor. I am happily married with two young children, and I take great delight in my family. I have lived the tough questions for a long time, and I relive those tough questions whenever I work with a battered woman of faith.

I have begun to live the answers, too. I believe in a God who stands with the oppressed, who hears their cries, and who moves in human history to end oppression and establish justice. I believe that Jesus suffered because he opposed institutionalized injustice and oppression. He was crucified by the people whose abusive power he undermined. Salvation came not because of Jesus' suffering and crucifixion, but because of God's decision to answer injustice, suffering, and death with new life. Our job as Christians is not to continue suffering and crucifixion but to establish new life, wholeness, and resurrection.[16]

8. Help people envision a world not yet seen, a world to live into.

I (Nora) once worked with a pastor whose leadership mantra was "Without vision, the people perish."[17] The same can be said of preaching. Without vision, sermons, too, will ultimately perish. Thus, a part of the preacher's sacred calling is to set before people an eschatological vision of a world they have not yet seen, but a world they are called to live into.

There are actually strong biblical precedents for this strategy, especially in the Hebrew prophets of old. Isaiah sets before a people in exile a vision of a peaceable kingdom, Jeremiah sets before a people whose hearts have been hardened the vision of a day when God's covenant would be written upon their hearts, and Ezekiel looks out upon a valley of dry and brittle bones and envisions a day when they will come to life through the Spirit's breath. Indeed, I am convinced that a part of the power of Martin Luther King's "I Have a Dream" speech is that King, like these prophets of old, not only called America on the carpet for our sins. He also gave us a vision to live into.

All too often, preaching can be quick to judge, but slow to give vision. Yet judgment alone will not take a sermon home. We also need its counterpart—prophetic vision—to help break through our resistances and embrace the new reality God has in store for us.[18]

EXERCISE: SERMONIC STRATEGIES FOR OVERCOMING RESISTANCE

Take one of the congregational resistances you named in the homiletical exercise in chapter 13, and make notes about how a sermon on this biblical passage (Micah 6, John 5, or Ephesians 4) might address it by means of one of the strategies discussed in this chapter. You may wish to combine strategies. For example, strategies 3 and 4 often work well together, as do 5 and 6. The eight strategies and the biblical texts are listed below for your convenience.

Strategies

1. Stand with the people under the word of God, rather than opposite the people armed with the word of God.

2. Re-contextualize the passage.

3. Start with the familiar and comfortable and move toward the unfamiliar to help the congregation stretch toward what is new.

4. Honor what people consider sacred and beautiful, and use it as a source of transformative power.

5. Use a congregation's own history as a connecting point to stretch the congregation.

6. Start with broader church or world history.

7. Use personal stories or testimonies to help humanize larger social or theological issues.

8. Help people envision a world not yet seen, a world to live into.

The Biblical Texts

Micah 6:6–8

"With what shall I come before
   the Lord,
    and bow myself before God on high?
Shall I come before him with
   burnt offerings,
   with calves a year old?
Will the Lord be pleased with
   thousands of rams,
   with ten thousands of rivers of oil?
Shall I give my firstborn for my
   transgression,
   the fruit of my body for the sin of my soul?"
He has told you, O mortal, what
   is good;

and what does the Lord require of you
but to do justice and to love
kindness,
and to walk humbly with your God?

John 5:1–9

After this there was a festival of the Jews, and Jesus went up to Jerusalem. Now in Jerusalem by the Sheep Gate there is a pool, called in Hebrew Beth-zatha, which has five porticoes. In these lay many invalids—blind, lame, and paralyzed. One man was there who had been ill for thirty-eight years. When Jesus saw him lying there and knew that he had been there a long time, he said to him, "Do you want to be made well?" The sick man answered him, "Sir, I have no one to put me into the pool when the water is stirred up; and while I am making my way, someone else steps down ahead of me." Jesus said to him, "Stand up, take your mat and walk." At once the man was made well, and he took up his mat and began to walk.

Ephesians 4:1–6

I therefore, the prisoner in the Lord, beg you to lead a life worthy of the calling to which you have been called, with all humility and gentleness, with patience, bearing with one another in love, making every effort to maintain the unity of the Spirit in the bond of peace. There is one body and one Spirit, just as you were called to the one hope of your calling, one Lord, one faith, one baptism, one God and Father of all, who is above all and through all and in all.

For Further Reflection/Discussion

Discuss your strategy with a small group, then with the class as a whole.

Notes

1. For a fuller discussion of Paul Tillich's understanding of "genuine" and "false" stumbling blocks, see Leonora Tubbs Tisdale, *Preaching as Local Theology and Folk Art* (Minneapolis: Fortress Press, 1997), 34–35.

2. For further discussion of this strategy, see Tisdale, *Preaching as Local Theology and Folk Art*, 50–51, and Leonora Tubbs Tisdale, *Prophetic Preaching: A Pastoral Approach* (Louisville, KY: Westminster John Knox Press, 2010), 49–51.

3. Walter Brueggemann, "The Preacher, Text, and People," *Theology Today* 47 (October 1990): 237–47.

4. Brian K. Blount, "Stay Close," in *Preaching Mark in Two Voices*, by Brian K. Blount and Gary V. Charles (Louisville, KY: Westminster John Knox Press, 2002), 170–80. Blount, who was on the faculty of Princeton Theological Seminary when he first preached this sermon, is currently president of Union Presbyterian Seminary in Virginia.

5. For this strategy, I am indebted to Barbara Lundblad, who first discussed it and used the James Forbes sermon example to illustrate it in her book *Transforming the Stone: Preaching through Resistance to Change* (Nashville: Abingdon Press, 2001), 53–55. It is also discussed in Tisdale, *Prophetic Preaching*, 44–46.

6. James A. Forbes Jr., a paraphrase from a videotaped sermon, as quoted in Lundblad, *Transforming the Stone*, 53–54.

7. This strategy is also discussed in Tisdale, *Prophetic Preaching*, 51–53.

8. William Sloane Coffin Jr., "Warring Madness," in *The Riverside Preachers*, ed. Paul H. Sherry (Cleveland, OH: Pilgrim Press, 1978), 154–59. The sermon was preached at The Riverside Church in New York City on May 21, 1978.

9. Sojourner Truth, "Modern History Sourcebook: Sojourner Truth: 'Ain't I a Woman?,' December 1851," accessed July 6, 2013, http://www.fordham.edu/halsall/mod/sojtruth-woman.asp.

10. Geoffrey Webber, *North German Church Music in the Age of Buxtehude* (New York: Oxford University Press, 1996), 14.

11. Ibid., 16.

12. The sermon was preached by Susan Murtha and Sharon Cody at First Congregational Church in Guilford, Connecticut, February 24, 2008.

13. Anne Marie Hunter, "Manna in the Wilderness," in *Telling the Truth: Preaching about Sexual and Domestic Violence*, ed. John S. McClure and Nancy J. Ramsay (Cleveland, OH: United Church Press, 1998), 136–40.

14. Hunter, "Manna in the Wilderness," 137.

15. Ibid., 139.

16. Ibid., 140.

17. Proverbs 29:18

18. This strategy is also discussed in Tisdale, *Preaching as Local Theology and Folk Art*, 119–21.

chapter 15

SERMON DELIVERY OPTIONS

We have used the word "delivery" in this chapter's title because it is common parlance for speaking of a sermon, but we are not pleased with the term. It is too anemic to capture what ideally happens when a preacher preaches effectively. "Delivery" suggests that the preacher is handing on a sermon that exists independently of the preacher's own self, as if she or he were delivering us a piece of furniture or a package that someone else had shipped to us.

Phillips Brooks, in his classic homiletical work *Lectures on Preaching*, drew on the metaphor of a delivery boy to explain what preaching is not. Writing in the nineteenth century, before the advent of mass electronic communication, Brooks pointed out that a delivery boy who brought a message to your door did not know what was in the message. He was merely the one who carried it to you. The messenger was unaware whether it was news that would make you rejoice or lament. Brooks observes that we do not want a preacher to be someone who impassively hands a message to us. We want someone who is thoroughly invested in the good news of God's love for us, someone who is stirred to the depth of his or her being by the grace of Jesus Christ, someone who is alive with the Holy Spirit, someone with a passion for the truth he or she is declaring to us.

In recent years, a number of homiletical scholars have formulated vivid new ways of understanding how the preaching of a sermon is more than the delivery of a message. Lucy Lind Hogan observes that preaching a sermon "is a way of thinking and of being before the Lord."[1] Then, drawing on the work of Jana Childers, Hogan identifies the qualities of personal presence that characterize thinking and being before the Lord: "passion, life, authenticity, naturalness, conviction, sincerity, . . . animation, . . . fire, sparks, electricity, mojo, spiritual lava, or juice."[2]

Mitties McDonald de Champlain succinctly summarizes why a preacher's vocal and visual presence are worthy of our close attention: "A central fact of the preaching life is that the sight and sound of the preacher are themselves carriers of meaning. The challenge, then, for every preacher is how and in what ways to become a fully embodied communicator when preaching."[3] Instead of being a messenger who delivers some information that has not noticeably affected ourselves, we want to be "fully embodied communicators," preachers whose voice, face, and gestures are congruent with the word we declare, whose very way of being, speaking, and doing incarnate the gospel we proclaim.

J. Alfred Smith reminds us of the hard work that is required if a sermon is going to become more than words on a page. His words are reminiscent of the biblical scene in which the prophet Jeremiah eats the scroll so that the word of God (literally) becomes a part of him:[4]

Before the sermon manuscript is ready for delivery, I must internalize the sermon so that it will be alive in my heart and active in my memory. A written manuscript is not ready for preaching. The material on the paper must take up residence in both the cognitive and affective dimensions of the soul of the preacher. This calls for serious communion with the sermon so that it is not a separate entity apart from the preacher. The sermon should soak the soul of the preacher, until it has become a part of the preacher. The sermon is the preacher and the preacher is the sermon. The sermon is not a speech the preacher has written. The sermon is the essence of who the preacher is and what the preacher believes.[5]

There is a lot at stake in sermon delivery. If our speech communication is such that people can't hear or understand what we are saying, if our heads are buried in manuscripts and people feel that we are distanced from them, if our facial and bodily expressions are at odds with the message we are bringing—then all our hard efforts in sermon preparation may well be undermined in the preaching moment. On the other hand, much is to be gained by a lively, engaging, heartfelt delivery. James Earl Massey puts the challenge to us this way:

> Those who experience our pulpit ministry will perceive something in connection with us. Will they perceive a caring that includes them? Will they perceive an evident scholarship, richly blended with deep reverence? Will they sense both a love for truth and a warmth for persons—a spirit of inclusiveness reflected in the conscious use of non-sexist language? When we stand to preach we *show* something along with what we *say*. We cause our hearers to *feel* as well as to *hear* something. What will it be?[6]

There is no single formula or method for achieving excellence in sermon delivery. For one thing, "How we speak, how we move, how we deliver our sermon are all culturally determined. One has only to attend several different worship services—Roman Catholic, Presbyterian, African American Baptist, a megachurch praise service—to realize that the performance style of one community will not necessarily work in another."[7]

It would be helpful at this point to identify the ways preachers are expected to speak, gesture, and use their bodies in your particular tradition. Here are three questions from chapter 2 worth reviewing or considering for the first time if you have skipped chapter 2:

> How do you expect preachers to use their voices? Is their vocal tone basically conversational, with the inflections of everyday speech but not a large dynamic range? Do you expect there to be considerable variation in the pace and volume of the speaking voice: for example, building or decreasing in volume as the sermon develops?
>
> How do you expect preachers to use their bodies? Do they sit or stand? Do they move a great deal, using many gestures? Do they remain basically still? Do they use direct eye contact or avert the eyes? Are they in a pulpit or the chancel or walking among the congregation or _____?
>
> To what extent do you expect preachers to express outwardly and freely their emotions? How much self-disclosure is expected of the preacher: none, some, a lot? Do you expect primarily an appeal to the heart or the mind or both?

Despite the variety of cultural expectations about how preachers will speak and move, we have found one commonality that appears to reach across the many traditions with which we have worked. In each tradition, there are some preachers who preach from a complete manuscript, some who speak from notes, and some who use no written materials at all. In each tradition, we have learned that whether or not a preacher is a fully embodied communicator is not a function of having a manuscript or notes or no notes. Some manuscript preachers look incessantly down at their papers, sending their voices primarily into the pulpit rather than the congregation as they read on and on in a voice with almost no tonal variation. But other manuscript preachers have clearly absorbed what they have written into the marrow of their bones. They may be reading, but we receive their sermon as a word spoken from their hearts to our hearts. They are fully embodied communicators.

The results are just as varied among those who use notes or no notes at all. Some wander about with no clear aim in sight, their transitions in thought either impossible to untangle or non-existent.

But others draw us into a sense of adventure and wonder as we follow them through carefully prepared shifts in thought and insight into the depths of God's Word. They are fully embodied communicators.

What the disembodied communicators share in common is their seeming lack of engagement with what they are telling us. They are like Phillip Brooks's messenger boys of the nineteenth century. They have something to give us, but it does not seem to matter to them. What the fully embodied communicators convey is a sense of urgency, excitement, delight, awe, wonder, astonishment at a truth that is so much larger than themselves yet as close to them as breath and pulse and as precious as life itself.

I, Tom, preach without notes or a manuscript. Although this method is not for everyone, I have had many students and preachers ask me how they might learn to preach without notes. I have first taught them the oral/aural style of writing that we describe in detail in the next chapter. Once they have mastered that and feel genuinely comfortable with it, I suggest they try reducing the amount they write. For example, if they are going to tell a story that is in their bones, I tell them to write down the word "story about _____" and the sentence that leads into the story and the sentence that leads to the next portion of the sermon. Over time, they get freer and freer from paper in their sermons. Preachers come to trust what is already written on their hearts, needing only the transitions to keep the sermon coherent and moving clearly toward its goal. Once preachers have mastered this method, they can often get a full-length sermon down to one or two pages of aural/oral writing. They are effectively outlining their sermon "moves." (For a fuller discussion of "moves," see discussion of David Buttrick in chapter 10). From that point, many eventually use no notes at all. They are not preaching extemporaneously or spontaneously, nor are they memorizing their sermons word for word. Instead, they are preparing their hearts and minds by reviewing and refining their sermons, preaching them aloud again and again to themselves. They spend as much time in preparation, if not more, as when they wrote out full manuscripts.

You do not need to preach without notes, but if it becomes something you want to develop, this will at least give you a method for working toward the goal.

I, Nora, preach from a manuscript. I started this practice early in my ministry, and I confess that after many years of using one, the manuscript has become my "security blanket" in the pulpit. I don't, however, read my sermon from the manuscript. I preach it. In order to help me to do so with maximum eye contact and freedom from the manuscript, I do several practical things. First, I outline the moves within the sermon with a word or a phrase in the left-hand margin of the manuscript so that I can glance down quickly and tell where I am on the page. Second, I highlight key words or phrases within the sermon manuscript in bold print so that they stand out on the page. Finally, I use subheadings—similar to the subheadings you would find in a book—to signal when major shifts from one move to the next take place.

Nothing, however, substitutes for practice, practice, practice. When I am writing a sermon, I frequently stop and read it to myself to see if it flows well in oral speech. If it doesn't, I know I'll also have trouble preaching it. The day before I preach, I usually go over my sermon at least two or three times in order to internalize it. Early on the day I am to preach, I actually preach the sermon out loud at least two or three more times, ideally in a private space where nobody interrupts me. On occasion, I've preached outside to the birds and squirrels, like St. Francis! Like Tom, I find that the easiest place to break free of the manuscript altogether is when telling stories. Strong beginnings and strong endings are also important to me, so I try to be comfortable enough with those portions of my sermon so that I can preach them without looking down at all.

I think the most important thing for me is to preach from the heart: to become familiar enough with the manuscript so that I can "tell" the sermon, giving honest and faithful testimony to what I believe.

Whether using a manuscript or notes or no notes, all preachers face the challenge of becoming "fully embodied communicators" of the word of God. There are methods of public speaking that can help move us toward this goal: standing solidly on both feet and getting well centered in our bodies before we begin, supporting our breath from the diaphragm, speaking clearly, varying the pace, taking adequate pauses, allowing the musicality of speech to find expression in how we inflect our voices, being in touch with the emotive contours of what we are saying. If you want to know more about the basics of speech communication for preaching, two helpful books are Jana Childers's *Performing the Word*[8] and G. Robert Jacks's *Getting the Word Across*.[9] If you want to place these works within the larger framework of performance studies and see how the principles of good performance can help you embody God's Word more completely, consider Richard F. Ward, *Speaking of the Holy: The Art of Communication in Preaching*.[10]

As helpful as these books are, methods alone will never make us "fully embodied communicators" of the word. Preaching is more than public speaking. It is a sacred action, a human being giving witness to the wonder of God. It involves what our African-American sisters and brothers call "soul." We find their use of that word very helpful when they speak of a musician singing with "soul" or a preacher preaching with "soul." Soul involves both emotion and intellect working in concert together. We might define soul this way: it is the wholeness of the human creature animated by the living Spirit of God. It is a wholeness that reaches out to others as people of profound worth. Teresa Fry Brown explains: "The essence of *soul* is to honor the value of all persons, regardless of who they are, where they live, how they look, or what they believe. [Margaret Goss] Burroughs writes that 'humanity and head and heart' are critical elements of our existence . . . [as] *soulfolk*."[11]

Understood this way, "soul" protects preachers from thinking that they are "fully embodied communicators" of God's Word simply because they are able to touch people's feelings. The liturgical theologian Don Saliers has pointed out that "a culture of hype makes it difficult to know the difference between feeling it now and the depth of emotion over time. . . . Our tropism is to go after immediacy. Our deeper desire is to be formed in a way that allows us to be grasped by a passion that takes us over time."[12] This profounder passion is part of what we mean by "soul."

The reality to which "soul" points is sometimes expressed in other cultures by other words. For example, I, Tom, recall hearing a lecture/sermon presentation by the Welsh homiletician Gwynn Walters more than thirty years ago in which he talked about the preacher's "song." "Every effective preacher," Walters said, "has a song." By "song," he did not mean literally a musical piece that the preacher sang. Rather, he referred to the musicality of the preacher's language and vocal inflection, to the way it suggested the heights and depths of wonder, the soaring and probing of the Spirit, the mystery evident in the sound that came from not just the vocal chords but the sacred chambers of heart.

Call it "soul," call it "song"—this wondrous quality is not something instantly acquired. The skills and arts that we explore in this book are essential to being a fully embodied communicator, but the technical mastery of them does not add up to having soul in one's preaching. Soul has to be nurtured by tending to the deepest wells of the Spirit within us and around us. Soul requires the discipline of homiletics plus the discipline of prayer. We attend to the living God whose Spirit prays in us and with us and through us in "sighs too deep for words" (Romans 8:26):

> Search and sound our mind and heart,
> Breath and Flame and Wind and Dove,
> let your prayer in us impart
> strength to do the work of love.[13]

EXERCISE: SERMON DELIVERY

1. Think of a preacher you have heard whose vocal and visual presence gave his or her preaching "soul," made him or her a "fully embodied communicator" of the word of God. Describe to yourself or a classmate your experience of the impact of hearing and seeing that preacher.

2. What things would most help you to develop "soul" in your preaching, to become a "fully embodied communicator" of the word of God? What might block you from attaining this goal?

Notes

1. Lucy Lind Hogan, *Graceful Speech: An Invitation to Preaching* (Louisville, KY: Westminster John Knox Press, 2006), 174.

2. Ibid. Lind Hogan is quoting from *Performing the Word: Preaching as Theatre*, by Jana Childers (Nashville: Abingdon Press, 1998), 18.

3. Mitties McDonald de Champlain, "What to Do While Preaching," in *Best Advice for Preaching*, ed. John S. McClure (Minneapolis: Fortress Press, 1998), 99–100.

4. See Jeremiah 15:16.

5. J. Alfred Smith Sr., "How Can They Hear without a Preacher?" in *Power in the Pulpit: How America's Most Effective Black Preachers Prepare Their Sermons*, ed. Cleophus J. LaRue (Louisville, KY: Westminster John Knox Press, 2002), 138.

6. James Earl Massey, *The Burdensome Joy of Preaching* (Nashville: Abingdon Press, 1998), 40.

7. Lind Hogan, *Graceful Speech*, 175.

8. Childers, *Performing the Word*.

9. G. Robert Jacks, *Getting the Word Across: Speech Communication for Pastors and Lay Leaders* (Grand Rapids, MI: Wm. B. Eerdmans Publishing Co., 1995).

10. Richard F. Ward, *Speaking of the Holy: The Art of Communication in Preaching* (St. Louis, MO: Chalice Press, 2001).

11. Teresa L. Fry Brown, *God Don't Like Ugly: African American Women Handing on Spiritual Values* (Nashville: Abingdon Press, 2000), 117.

12. Don Saliers, presentation at the Congregations Projects conference of the Yale Institute of Sacred Music, June 27, 2012.

13. Thomas H. Troeger, "Through Our Fragmentary Prayers," in *Borrowed Light: Hymn Texts, Prayers and Poems* (New York: Oxford University Press, 1994), 123.

part two

WRITING LIKE A PREACHER

ORAL/AURAL SPEECH FOR PREACHING

The exercises in Part II of this book are designed to help you learn to write like a preacher. This style of writing is different from academic writing in several respects.

First, while academic writing requires extensive footnoting and a logical thought progression in which the author makes one sustained and defensible argument—often in order to convince the reader of the validity of his or her point of view—the aims of sermon writing are more varied. St. Augustine summarized it well in his fifth-century treatise on preaching when he wrote that the goals of preaching should be "to teach, to delight, and to persuade" in order that the gospel be heard "intelligently, willingly, and obediently."[1] Sermons not only aim for persuasion; they also aspire to "teach" congregations about the Bible, theology, and the nature of the faith; to "delight" them with rhetoric and language that engages their imaginations and their intellects and makes them eager to follow a sermon to its end; and to "persuade" and move the hearer toward a change in belief, attitude, or action. According to Augustine, in good preaching, the head, the heart, and the will are all engaged. Consequently, preaching calls for a style of writing that utilizes vivid imagery, engaging narrative, and the imaginative use of language that is often more evidenced in good literary writing or poetry than in academic papers.

Second, unlike academic writing, crafting sermons requires that we write for the ear as opposed to the eye, and that we become acquainted with the particular cadences and rhythms of oral speech. Many homileticians have stressed how a sermon is far more than what the preacher has written down. Justo González is "very much disturbed when people speak of a piece of paper or a manuscript as a 'sermon.' A sermon is not a text. A sermon is an event. In that event, the text—whether written, outlined, or completely oral—is just one element. And I am not convinced that it is always the most important element!"[2] In a similar manner, Zan Holmes expresses the eventful quality of preaching by asserting that "the major task of the preacher is to enable the Word of God to *happen again* for the preacher and the congregation."[3]

In order for a sermon to happen, in order for it to be an act or event, the preacher must have what Gardner Taylor describes as "a natural feel for the essential music of the English language wedded to an intimate and emotional affection for the great transactions of the Scriptures."[4] There is perhaps no greater example of the "essential music" of effective preaching than the sermons of Martin Luther King Jr., as he delivered them. Richard Lischer describes how Martin Luther King Jr.'s voice moved his audience: "The gradual ascendancy of his pitch from a low growl at the beginning of the sermon to a piercing shout at the upper range of his high baritone, the predictable rhythm of the rise and fall of his voice, and the relentless increase in the *rate* of his speech—all contribute to the melodiousness, the songlike quality, of his voice."[5]

Experienced preachers, even if they use a full manuscript, know how important it is that they adequately rehearse their sermons because "the inflection of one's voice determines the meaning of words written on a page."[6] Thus Prathia L. Hall writes, "The pronunciation, intonation, rhythm, and sing-song modulations in my voice can only be captured by the voice, not by the mere choice of words. Yet my repetition of certain words and phrases gives greater power and effectiveness to voicing themes of suffering and celebration. This is important to facilitating a 'listening' imagination."[7]

In order to engage the "listening imagination," our writing needs to be more conversational in style, employing shorter phrases and avoiding complicated sentences with a number of dependent clauses. A format for this style of writing follows. Note that each line contains only one brief phrase, and that sentences, on the whole, are shorter than if we were writing an analytical, academic essay.

Write like this for the ear:

Not the long sentences of written prose.
But brief sentences.
Words and clauses.
Each one getting a line.

This is the way we talk.
The way we listen.
How we hear.
Develop your ear for speech.
How words are heard.
Or lip read.

Now and then, you can get away with a longer sentence such as the one you are reading at this moment.

But.
That's for the eye.
Not the ear.
It makes for hard listening.

And it makes for getting lost while preaching!
Tangled language
becomes tangled revelation,
an obstacle course
for the congregation,
for the heart hungering for God.

Short lines
are easier to follow.
Especially
if you're nervous.

Play around with this method.
Play with language.
Play with different ways of thinking.
Of seeing.
Of being.
Of communicating.

Kind of fun—
isn't it?
It will open you to the Spirit.
And your congregation too!

Writing sermons this way allows preachers to look up and out upon the congregation more often, and then easily locate their place on the page as they return to the manuscript. This keeps the flow of energy more between the preacher and the congregation than between the preacher and the page. This is a significant matter. It influences the reception of the sermon because listeners read the faces of preachers as well as listen to their words. Preachers buried in their manuscripts are diminishing the delight of interpersonal communication that is part of the power of preaching.

In all of the exercises that follow in Part II, we ask that you use the oral/aural style of writing, keeping the length of the assignment to only one double-spaced page (12-point Times New Roman type). While we know it will be challenging at first, this discipline is a helpful one for preaching, in which clarity and brevity are often assets. If you find that your words are wandering across the page, or that you are spilling over onto a second page, go back and rework the exercise.

At the end of each chapter, we will provide some model exercises selected from papers that students have written in our introductory preaching course at Yale Divinity School over a number of years. We are publishing the students' work with their permission and hope that you will find them as inspiring as we have. Our own practice is to begin each class session in our introductory course by reading aloud anonymously the best four or five papers that were turned in the previous week. In this way, students have the opportunity both to learn from one another and to witness firsthand the amazing preaching gifts of their classmates.

We encourage you to think of these exercises as one-page "mini-sermons" that could be preached to a congregation or to a class of your peers. Some of you may want to incorporate portions of the exercises into the longer sermons you prepare or use them in settings where a brief meditation is required.

Whatever your ultimate use of them, please recognize that the goal of the exercises is to help you learn to write like a preacher. Our hope is that the skills and style of writing you learn through engaging them will also carry over into the writing of your full-length sermons.

Notes

1. St. Augustine, *On Christian Doctrine*, trans. D. W. Robertson Jr. (Indianapolis, IN: Bobbs-Merrill Educational Publishing, 1958), 142.

2. Justo L. González, "A Hispanic Perspective: By the Rivers of Babylon," in *Preaching Justice: Ethnic and Cultural Perspectives*, ed. Christine Marie Smith (Cleveland, OH: United Church Press, 1998), 80.

3. Zan Holmes, "Enabling the Word to Happen," in *Power in the Pulpit: How America's Most Effective Black Preachers Prepare Their Sermons*, ed. Cleophus J. LaRue (Louisville, KY: Westminster John Knox Press, 2002), 74.

4. Gardner C. Taylor, *How Shall They Preach* (Elgin, IL: Progressive Baptist Publishing House, 1977), 13.

5. Richard Lischer, *The Preacher King: Martin Luther King, Jr. and the Word That Moved America* (New York: Oxford University Press, 1995), 133. Cited in O. C. Edwards Jr., *A History of Preaching* (Nashville: Abingdon Press, 2004), 710.

6. Stephen H. Webb, *The Divine Voice: Christian Proclamation and the Theology of Sound* (Grand Rapids, MI: Brazos Press, 2004), 208.

7. Prathia L. Hall, "Encountering the Text," in *Power in the Pulpit*, 65.

IMAGES OF GOD IN EVERYDAY LIFE

In her book *The Preaching Life*, Barbara Brown Taylor recounts her growing-up years and the impact of her experience on her faith and understanding of God. She says even disappointments and disillusionments about God can become opportunities for new understanding: "Did God fail to come when I called? Then perhaps God is not a minion. So who is God? Did God fail to punish my adversary? Then perhaps God is not a policeman. So who is God? Did God fail to make everything turn out all right? Then perhaps God is not a fixer. So who is God?"[1]

Note the pattern of Brown Taylor's writing: she uses her experience to grow in the knowledge of God. She learns God is not a minion nor a policeman nor a fixer. But she also learns something profounder: that her experience keeps driving her to ask, "So who is God?"

Asian theologian Choa-Seng Song says that the stories that often speak to us most profoundly of God may not, on first impression, seem particularly "Christian" in nature. Indeed, some of them may come to us through life experiences that seem very secular on the surface, or through observing the lives of people who hold other religious beliefs. Song writes, "Literally countless stories, though unrelated to Christianity, are related to God. Do not these stories tell us Christians how they [people from other cultures] wrestle with the vicissitudes of life and how they strive to find in God the fulfillment of that life?"[2]

This dialogue between who we think God to be and our experience, a conversation that draws us deeper and deeper into the wonder and mystery of God, is an essential part of the life of faith both for individuals and for the church. It is a process that shapes preachers and their sermons and that informs the varied responses of listeners. Teresa Fry Brown reminds us that we bring these life experiences with us every time we interpret biblical texts for preaching. We do not approach Scripture with a blank slate, but with a treasure trove of experiences that have shaped our own images and understanding of God. Consequently, Fry Brown encourages us to "exegete" ourselves prior to entering into a conversation with biblical texts, asking ourselves questions like "What do I believe? Who is God in my life? What is my image of God?"[3]

One of the most important functions of preaching is to help people grow in the love and knowledge of God, and one of the best ways preachers can prepare for that task is to reflect on how this has happened to them. Write one double-spaced page oral/aural style about some crucial aspect of your experience that has shaped or reshaped your understanding of God.[4] In the pages that follow are some exercises that our students have written that may stimulate your own creative work.

Student Exercises

"Return it to the earth!" my pastor would say,
offering my little sister and me a linen cloth
wrapped around leftover communion bread.
Together we'd scamper outside
to a maple tree on the edge of the church parking lot.
Still a sacrament—still the Body of Christ, broken and blessed—
we scattered the crumbs at the base of the tree,
inviting the birds, yes, even the squirrels,
to join the Eucharistic Feast.

Some traditions would find this practice reproachable.
(Should not the elements be wholly consumed by the congregation?)
Others would wonder why we took such care with the crumbs.
(Isn't it but leftover bread from a meal that's over?)
As for me, the practice shaped in my young imagination,
an image of a God generous beyond measure.
An incarnate-God who came for the redemption of all that God had made.
Even the squirrels. Even the soil and earthworms. Even me.
As followers of this Jesus, we too are a Body leavened and living,
given to the whole creation
that it might taste and see the goodness of God.[5]

◇◇◇◇◇◇◇

Faith, for me, began with fear.

When I was eleven years old, I read the book Salem's Lot *by Stephen King.*
Don't ask me why my parents allowed this.
Stephen King is not a good idea for an eleven-year-old.
It terrified me.
Literally.
I was scared to be alone,
and I would have panic attacks if I was made to walk through the woods by myself.
What frightened me about the book, though, was not the evil it portrayed.
I knew it was horror, so I expected evil.
What I did not expect was the absence of good.
I found myself in a world in which pure evil existed,
but in which the "good guys" fighting it were selfish,
fallible, slightly lower-than-average, normal human beings.
No match for the evil.
I began to wonder if life was like that,
and that was what scared me.

There had to be good in the world,
and the only way I knew how to believe in a good pure enough
to counter that kind of evil was to believe in God.
The eleven-year-old's fundamental belief that God is good,
that God is the ultimate good,
is still at the foundation of my faith in God.[6]

I learned what it means to feel God love you through a congregation
while I attended a lively Caribbean British church
on the northwest side of London.
I arrived there only about eight weeks after my mother had passed away.
I felt utterly alone, living in a foreign country, thousands of miles from family.
But the members of the congregation loved on me.
Folks were not satisfied unless I was eating at their homes, fellowshipping at their tables,
laughing at their accents while they laughed at mine.
They would even check on me—
calling me and sending me text messages from their "MO-byles."
And, they were always glad to see me.
These simple acts of kindness—
these seemingly effortless acts of hospitality to the stranger—
illumined God's love for me when I was in utter despair.
Amazingly, only about three people knew
my grief and my need to be embraced by the community.
But God knew.
And God loved me through a congregation.[7]

Throughout the ages God has been speaking to us.
Through signs and visions. And through messengers.
We sometimes call these messengers angels.
As a child, my life was filled with pain.
Abuse and neglect. Nights of tears. Darkness.
In these dark nights, a messenger visited me.
The angel came with words of comfort and peace.
This angel was my Granny. She promised to be with me.
To see me through the night until morning breaks.
Above all, she simply loved me.
She spoke of God's unfailing love for me.
Granny was my Gabriel.
My messenger proclaiming in word and act, Love Incarnate.
Truly, God is there in our night times.
So then, hear the angel's voice among your tears.
"Behold, I bring tidings of great joy."
God is with us. Emmanuel is indeed in our midst.[8]

121

Notes

1. Barbara Brown Taylor, *The Preaching Life* (Plymouth, UK: Cowley Publications, 1993), 9.

2. Choan-Seng Song, "Preaching as Shaping Experience in a World of Conflict," in *Preaching as Shaping Experience in a World of Conflict,* ed. Prof. Dr. Albrecht Grözinger and Rev. Dr. Kang Ho Soon (Utrecht: Societas Homiletica, 2005), 32.

3. Teresa L. Fry Brown in *Purposes of Preaching*, ed. Jana Childers (St. Louis, MO: Chalice Press, 2004), 56.

4. See chapter 16 for instructions on writing in the oral/aural style.

5. Mary Emily Briehl Duba.

6. Emilie Aurora Finn.

7. Charrise Barron.

8. Blake Scalet.

CONGREGATIONS AS
PARTNERS IN PREACHING

Preaching may seem, at first, like a very solitary act, but in actuality, as James Earl Massey reminds us, preaching is a "partnership" that "proceeds best not from correct and fluent exegesis alone, but from a sensed camaraderie with the people in the need for grace and the hope of God's glory."[1] The sermon is born out of a lived and ongoing dialog with the congregation. This is why preaching is not something separated and isolated from the pastoral care of a congregation. Attending to the sick, the grieving, and those in any other need or adversity, and relishing the joys of life, conversation, and shared meals—all of these things and more are part of the fabric of preaching.

Eunjoo Mary Kim observes that the congregation can be an active contributor to the sermon in at least three ways. First, through its own lived experiences and faith journey, the congregation both preserves memories of God's action in its midst, and also raises existential and theological issues for ongoing reflection in preaching. Thus, it "functions like a homiletical treasury in which the preacher can gain theological and methodological insights into and implications for the proclamation of the Word of God." Second, the congregation actually participates in co-creating the sermon with the preacher. This process might take place through a group Bible study structured around the texts for an upcoming sermon, through the active involvement of congregants in the preaching of the sermon itself, or through the verbal and nonverbal feedback the congregation gives the preacher as the sermon is proclaimed. And finally, congregations "are the agents for fulfilling preaching. . . . Its members are a bridge connecting the Word of God proclaimed in a liturgical context to the larger context of society." In other words, without the congregation, the sermon would not come to fruition in the witness of Christians in the larger world.[2]

Eleazar Fernandez summarizes the relationship between preacher and congregation well when he says, "Preachers do not come from the outside pulling the people into the promised future, but they are companions in the journey."[3]

Write one page (double spaced, oral/aural style)[4] examining the implications of this understanding of preaching for how you will create, deliver, and evaluate your sermons over long periods of ministry. How do you make the congregation itself a part of your sermon process? In the pages that follow are some exercises that our students have written that may stimulate your own creative work.

Student Exercises

A sermon is not just a fifteen-minute opportunity to hear yourself speak.

It is not a time for a monologue.

Yes, you may be the only one speaking,

but if you are the only one whom you can hear,

then you're doing it wrong.

Rather, a sermon is simply one part of a conversation,

a conversation started in the waiting room of a hospital call

as you sit with the parents of a teenaged daughter who was hit by a drunk driver,

a conversation started by the story on the front page of the newspaper

about a murderer condemned to death in the courthouse just down the street,

a conversation started by the adoption of a child to an infertile couple,

and by the gay couple who was denied the right to adopt.

Preaching is supposed to

"comfort the afflicted and afflict the comfortable."

It is a time to share a prophetic imagination about the future,

while staying present with the grief and pain of those in the pews.

Preaching is about calling to action,

while making space for restorative and restful inaction.

How can any of us know how to do this

if we forget to listen to the other side of the conversation?[5]

The congregation and I

Preach together.

I hear the threads of their lives

In Bible study, coffee hour

And knit them into the sermon.

I try to connect our lives with scripture.

The Good News as tidings of today.

I learn to step out from behind the pulpit.

To stop clutching onto paper

so our hearts can speak to each other.

Is it working?

I will look for signs

that I have helped equip them for their ministry.

That each sees herself, himself

as God's person in the world.

As part of the priesthood of all believers.

But what does that look like?

Maybe like people empowered in the church.

Wearing their baptism as ordination.

Maybe like people who view their work as their vocation.

Wearing their day jobs like Geneva gowns.

Donning their parenting like albs.

Their ordinary activity wrapping them like stoles.
I listen for our worship becoming conversation.
And that we are interpreting together.[6]

On Tuesdays in college,
everyone drifted into evening Mass already wondering about Sunday.
In fall, we'd settle into a pile of leaves out back,
sometimes curl up around the fireplace in winter,
or lay flat on the cool chapel floor while the sun baked spring into summer.
Whatever it took to hear, really hear, the readings.
And then Father Gary would say: The Gospel Question is . . .
And we'd be off on some urgent quest or another!
. . . racing from St. Louis to Judea and back again
on some spiritual scavenger hunt of a homily.
I've never seen such a lively discussion or thorough exegesis anywhere else.
So many treasures brought back from the pilgrimage of a hundred inquiring hearts!
A true lectio divina.
And there on the altar, we'd dump our most acute metaphors, most interior revelations.
No need to hold onto them.
On Sunday, we knew, they'd reappear:
our discoveries marked in a homiletic atlas made of us but not by us.
For on Tuesdays in college, Father Gary sent us delving into ourselves
knowing that we'd bring him back the God residing there.
Not a bad strategy for finding gospel answers to gospel questions.
Or at the very least,
keeping us pondering til Sunday.[7]

When I am seventy
and the hair that tops my collar
is gray and wispy
I will open my desk and take out my file
a file full of scraps of paper.
Bar napkins; fine stationary; backs of envelopes
covered in fragments of thought
pieces of good news.
"Hope in the resurrection!"
cries the back of a gum wrapper.
Notes will be in the file too—
letters from parishioners
critiquing my 257th sermon.
Notes from friends,
praising my first.
But over the long arch of time,

Chapter 18

I will judge myself
not so much by the "good jobs"
or the "needs improvements,"
but by how near with words I draw to God
and who I take with me.[8]

Notes

1. James Earl Massey, *The Burdensome Joy of Preaching* (Nashville: Abingdon Press, 1998), 38.

2. Eunjoo Mary Kim, *Preaching the Presence of God: A Homiletic from an Asian American Perspective* (Valley Forge, PA: Judson Press, 1999), 11–13.

3. Eleazar S. Fernandez, "A Filipino Perspective: 'Unfinished Dream' in the Land of Promise," in *Preaching Justice: Ethnic and Cultural Perspectives,* ed. Christine Marie Smith (Cleveland, OH: United Church Press, 1998), 67.

4. See chapter 16 for instructions on writing in the oral/aural style.

5. Elizabeth Bonney.

6. Luanne Rose Panarotti. The unique way of using capitalization and punctuation are Panarotti's. Students sometimes do this to help themselves inflect their reading and take pauses in a way that makes their speaking more listenable.

7. Stephanie Wong.

8. Emily Wachner.

IMAGES THAT COMPETE FOR ALLEGIANCE IN OUR LIVES

Richard A. Jensen observes, "Preaching comes in three basic forms: thinking in idea, thinking in story, and the subject of [his] book: thinking in picture. Today's churchgoers, steeped in multimedia communications, have been trained to think and learn with their eyes and ears together."[1] Jensen insists that "we attend more to the visual character of our age in the preaching process. How can we make use of visualization in preaching for people who live in a strongly visual environment?"[2] These questions extend beyond homiletical method into the realm of values and ethics, for the "visual environment" that Jensen rightfully wants preachers to engage includes gratuitous violence and nurturing a culture of conspicuous consumption. All of us who live in this environment are bombarded with images trying to win our allegiance: images telling us what it means to be a success or a failure, images nurturing a desire for things we do not need, images of others different from ourselves, images of what the world is like or what it ought to become, images of God and creation, so many different images that preachers, too, must think in picture as well as in idea and story.

For Teresa Fry Brown, the process of re-visualizing the world is one of the chief functions of preaching: "The purpose of preaching is to visualize pregnant possibilities of transformation of individuals, communities, nations, and the world from depressed, debilitated, disenfranchised, disrespected, disinterested, destructive, and depreciated entities into constructive, conscientious, creative, cooperative, connected, confident, and Christlike beings."[3]

What images have competed for allegiance in your life? Which have you chosen and which have chosen you, perhaps overcoming your better judgment? What insight does this process give you into preaching to people who face the same struggle with competing images of self, others, world, and God? Write one page, double spaced, oral/aural style,[4] in which you reflect on these questions. In the pages that follow are some exercises that our students have written that may stimulate your own creative work.

Student Exercises

When I was in middle school,
I covered my walls with fashion magazine ads

127

colorful photographs of skinny white bodies
called beautiful,
worthy,
perfect.
I have been haunted all my life
by these images of perfection
that do not look like me
And never will.
But God is not the editor of Seventeen or Vogue.
He is not Hollywood or Madison Avenue.
I am in the glossy photographs
taped up on the walls of God's bedroom
I am the face God sees
when she looks in the mirror
Just as I am
Just as you are
Just as we all are
Perfect in every way
Just the way God made us.[5]

◇◇◇◇◇◇◇◇

"I'm a perfectionist,"
I used to explain with some amount of pride.
One day my dad asked me,
"Do you think that's a good thing?"
I've thought about his question often in the years since he posed it.
Is it good
to measure myself by a standard which is always
utterly unreachable?
Is it good to fear failure so much
that the thought of it brings on palpable,
paralyzing panic?
Is it good to live as though I must be one particular way,
or I will not be loved,
not really loved?
Is this not a sort of idolatry?
Haven't I turned
"perfection" into a god?
Haven't I set it before me
as the one thing that will make me worthy,
make me valuable,
the one thing that will save me?
Help me, Lord,
to know myself in you.

Teach me to seek after you,
rather than the image of my own perfection.[6]

For as long as I can remember,
my father has called me by the nickname "tiger."
I love the image of a tiger:
strong and sleek, powerful and graceful . . .
Even as a twenty-nine-year-old,
I feel the same unwitting twinge of glee
whenever (now less frequently) he refers to me as "tiger."
      At some point during college, however,
I began, somehow, to care far too much about
what other people (especially my father) thought of me.
I began to feel more like a kitten than a tiger.
      How is it that, overnight, we can become so darned afraid?
I wonder how many eagles among us
have been reduced to chickens,
how many dolphins made into minnows,
by the countless, internalized, accusatory voices of our culture
that tell us "no":
that we are not pretty, good, or smart enough?
It was not until last year,
when my father and I began grieving
my mother's second bout with cancer,
that I began to realize
that perhaps the closest I can ever come to understanding God's love on this earth
might be through experiencing a parent's—my father's—love for me.[7]

Notes

1. Richard A. Jensen, *Envisioning the Word: The Use of Visual Images in Preaching* (Minneapolis: Fortress Press, 2005), 5.

2. Ibid., 6.

3. Teresa L. Fry Brown, "The Action Potential of Preaching," in *The Purposes of Preaching*, ed. Jana Childers (St. Louis, MO: Chalice Press, 2004), 51–52.

4. See chapter 16 for instructions on writing in the oral/aural style.

5. M Adryael Tong.

6. Kelly Rich Klee.

7. W. Travis Helms.

BIBLICAL SCOUNDRELS AND TRICKSTERS

The Bible reveals not only the truth of God but also the truth about humanity, and it is not always attractive truth. To be sure, there is the glory of our being made in the image of God and the witness to the astounding tenacity of God's love, but there is also the long, bloody, messy story of betrayal and violence that starts with Adam and Eve, Cain and Abel, and all who follow them. As a colorful character in one of Paul Theroux's novels describes the Bible: "It's the truth about what people do. They cuss. They kill their childrens. They do wrongness. They suffer for years and years and they look around and suffer some more. And sometimes nothing happens for two-three hundred years but begetting."[1] Scoundrels and tricksters and just plain evil folk parade through the Bible, and yet somehow God works with and through such people. When our ancient forebears told their sacred stories, they did not hide the family secrets like skeletons in the closet. They left them in plain sight, a witness to the truth that God works through fallible human beings, a revelation that gives hope to *us* fallible human beings, and to our world of betrayal and violence.

Select any one biblical character who is more a scoundrel or trickster than a saint and, in one page (double spaced, oral/aural style),[2] describe how God works through her or him. In the pages that follow are some exercises that our students have written that may stimulate your own creative work.

Student Exercises

It took a long time for Jacob to trust God.
He always felt compelled to grab what he needed:
His brother's heel; his brother's birthright.
Jacob wrestled directly with God and grabbed at a blessing
When the weaker and more obedient wouldn't have even gone to the mat.
It seems God would prefer a rule-follower,
A saccharine-sweet, trusting soul who meekly says, "Yes, Lord,"
And waits for God to act.
But Jacob's story speaks to those of us who aren't so sweet,
Those who haven't always waited on God.
We smile slyly about the meek ones.

While they're in the waiting room, we see God face to face.
They say they have too much faith to ask the questions.
Jacob and I say we have enough faith to ask them.
I'd rather see God face to face in a wrestling match than not at all.
Besides, from the outside, wrestling looks just like embracing.
I know Jacob. I am Jacob.
Sure, we sneaked in the back door.
But Jacob and I refuse to let go. We have met God.
We have the limp to prove it. We wear it like a badge. [3]

I'll be the first to admit it.
I screen my calls.
All the time.
But I'm in pretty good company.
A whole lot of biblical prophets screened their calls.
Jonah is my favorite—
the one who didn't just hit the reject button,
but bought a one-way ticket to the edge of the world.
Still, God's call is one that must be answered eventually.
Jonah,
call screener extraordinaire,
couldn't even avoid it by getting himself thrown overboard into the sea.
Yet,
for all his resistance to God's call,
despite his best efforts to run and fail,
Jonah's single-sentence oracle transforms a corrupt city and fulfills God's purpose.
In a world filled with call screeners like me,
I'm encouraged to know that God will get through eventually
and overcome resistance to bring about God's will in our world. [4]

If Rahab the prostitute had been an Israelite,
she would have been declared one of the worst figures in the Bible.
She betrays her people,
puts her trust in the might of foreign kingdoms
instead of her own ancestral gods,
acts as a spy to save only her own family
from the destruction of her city.
But she is from Jericho.
She helps Joshua's men to extend the rule of Israelites,
she professes the fear that even foreigners have of the Lord,
and earns a place in the genealogy of Jesus.
Does she send the disturbing message
that evil is no longer evil if it is for the sake of the Lord?

Or that women are naturally treacherous,
and God uses what tools he can?
I have no satisfactory answer.
But perhaps the story of Rahab is meant to unsettle us
subverting our expectations in the midst of genocidal nationalism
and placing the responsibility for Israel's success
not in its own warriors
but in the hands of a foreign woman.
Why does Israel think its military victories prove its worth?[5]

◇◇◇◇◇◇◇

Mirrors are odd.
If you think about it
Some people have never seen what they look like
Until one day—BAM!
Their own face
Every deep contour
Opens like a new story before them.
I can remember the first time
I saw myself reflected back to me
It was not the first time I got a haircut
Or when I peered over the edge to glimpse the smooth lake surface
It was the first time I heard Peter deny Jesus.
He was supposed to be the rock, the foundation.
Yet he betrays Jesus. Three times.
The first disciple to proclaim Jesus as Messiah turns his back
Peter's failure to acknowledge the man he had changed his life to follow
Mirrored for me the ways I daily deny my Lord and my God.
But the Good News remains
In John's gospel we still hear of Peter, running to the tomb
Still urgent in his belief that maybe the tomb will be empty
And he will get another chance and this time
He will say "Yes, Lord" and mean it.[6]

Notes

1. Paul Theroux, *Picture Palace* (Boston: Houghton Mifflin Company, 1978), 96.
2. See chapter 16 for instructions on writing in the oral/aural style.
3. Carol Mead.
4. Javen Swanson.
5. Clara Coughlin.
6. Bethany Leigh Myers.

TAKING PART IN AN EXPERIENCE OF GOD'S LIVING WORD

Barbara Brown Taylor writes, "Once I have done all my homework and have a decent idea what the text means, I give it a rest. Understanding is not enough. I do not want to pass on knowledge from the pulpit; I want to take part in an experience of God's living word, and that calls for a different kind of research."[1] Taylor is avoiding the gnostic heresy: the belief that ideas and understanding alone save us. It is a temptation to which we preachers can easily succumb because, as Anna Carter Florence says, "[W]e were trained to talk *about* the text: to explain it, or solve it, or hunt down its one true 'meaning.' We were trained to study and conjugate and translate into key theological ideas, and we can do it all day if you let us. We can keep talking about that text until the road is clogged with more information than one sermon can handle."[2]

Ideas and understanding are obviously important. But consider the difference between having ideas about how to parent children, and actually being a parent; the difference between ideas about justice and actually getting a piece of legislation passed that brings more justice; or the difference between an idea for the church's mission and actually carrying it out effectively. It is the experience, the embodiment, the incarnation of the idea that brings the truth home to you, and that holds for sermons as much as any other human endeavor. The gospel is about the Word not just being an idea, but becoming flesh, and, as Franciska Stark reminds us, "Preaching is part of the living Word itself. Preaching bears the promise that one can get in contact with the presence of the living God through the power of the Holy Spirit."[3]

Write one page (double spaced, oral/aural style)[4] in which you recount an experience you have had of God's living word. In the pages that follow are some exercises that our students have written that may stimulate your own creative work.

Student Exercises

It's been a hummingbird summer.
The Roses of Sharon have grown up thickly around the deck
providing a haven from the eyes of hawks that circle high overhead.
Sitting side by side in green resin chairs,
we halt our conversation

when the hummingbirds swoop in like Cessnas under the awning,
their wings humming like finely tuned engines.
Don't move! Don't make a sound!
We hold our breath as one sips nectar at a blossom
and share a smile of wonder out of the corners of our eyes.
The surprise of their arrival is matched
by the suddenness of their departure.
Delightful grace comes in at the corners of our hearts.
Its appearance cannot be timed or scheduled or demanded.
But it will come,
so we sit and wait
and listen for the sound of its wings.[5]

You have heard of singing in the shower,
but what about preaching there, too?

I like to think that I do my best thinking in the shower,
but that is because the shower is where there are only thoughts.
There can be no books and no notes,
nowhere for distractions or doubts to hide.

In the shower, there is only water:
water that washes old ideas away,
water that marks the boundary between the past and the present,
water that makes a seam between the yesterday and the today.

But water is never only water:
every bath is like the *bath,*
even the shower can be a remembrance of baptism.

So let every sermon have at least a few showers,
and there will be time for the words to be baptized,
space for the Word to come alive.

Let every sermon have at least a few showers,
and that sermon will sing of the Lord.[6]

Baptized by immersion when I was eleven years old,
I had no idea what it really meant to be adopted by God,
to be buried with Christ in the water of baptism,
and to share in Christ's resurrection.
All I knew was that Christ was calling to me and wanted me to follow him.
Hidden among the people who were standing and singing in the church pews

I slipped out into the center aisle.
My heart was pounding as I walked toward the minister
who stood beneath the giant wooden cross that hung from the ceiling.
I felt like I was on the strings of a puppeteer
who was helping me put one foot in front of the other.
My body was covered in goose bumps and I was afraid I was going to trip and fall.
I was scared but I kept hearing everyone around me belt out the hymn,
Blessed Assurance, Jesus Is Mine!
I changed into a white robe and entered the water.
The minister helped me bend backward,
and for a brief moment,
I heard only silence when my head went under water.
Then the minister pulled me up and welcomed me
as I took my first breath in my new life in Christ.
I had been marked as Christ's own forever.[7]

You all know the one about the mustard seed,
that mighty bush, those birds of the air.
Just leave that for now.
Come fly with me
to Austin, Texas, to the Episcopal Mission of El Buen Samaritano.
The heat slaps your face like a steaming dishrag as you step down from our bus.
But notice these five low buildings:
the bright ochre of the walls, those pristine pantiled roofs,
this grass, those shady colonnades.
A sign greets you, the honored guest, by name, and gets the spelling right.
Take it all in while our bus door gasps shut behind you,
but not before the driver tells you that once there was nothing here at all.
You want to dip your hand in that fountain, but we don't have time.
Father Ed Gomez has come out to greet you, has called you by name
and leads you now down hallways tiled with cool terra cotta.
This clinic logged eight thousand visits last year, all uninsured.
ESL classes, says Father Ed, help eleven hundred clients help themselves.
This pantry, walls painted a welcoming celery, fed fourteen hundred last month.
Baker's racks of stainless steel proffer tuna, rice, tomatoes, chilies.
Once, in 1990, there was nothing here at all.
El Buen Samaritano was a basement closet in a downtown church.
But now it welcomes you, me, and the people of this city—
all the birds of the air—
by name.[8]

Notes

1. Barbara Brown Taylor, *The Preaching Life* (Plymouth, UK: Cowley Publications, 1993), 81–82.
2. Anna Carter Florence, *Preaching as Testimony* (Louisville, KY: Westminster John Knox Press, 2007).

3. Franciska Stark, "Empirical Research in the Field of Homiletics: Asking for the Hearers' Voice," in *Preaching as Shaping Experience in a World of Conflict*, ed. Prof. Dr. Albrecht Grözinger and Rev. Dr. Kang Ho Soon (Utrecht: Societas Homiletica, 2005), 91.

4. See chapter 16 for instructions on writing in the oral/aural style.

5. Lucy Driscoll LaRocca.

6. Casey N. Cep.

7. Dawn M. Stegelmann.

8. Patrick Carroll Ward.

SHIFTING THE POINT OF VIEW

David Buttrick has observed, "We are now moving out of an age in which rational objectivity was the order of the day in pulpit discourse . . . rather clearly, twentieth-century consciousness has changed. Reality for modern men and women is much more than a world 'out there'—consciousness is perspectival."[1] Buttrick wrote these words more than twenty-five years ago, but they are truer now than when he first penned them. The intensified attention that theology has given to culture, class, gender, and race in shaping our beliefs and practices has made our consciousness even more "perspectival." We have an ever-increasing awareness that how we see the world depends immensely on where we stand. The same principle holds for how we see a passage in the Bible: where we stand in the passage and what characters we focus on and what characters we ignore will tremendously shape our interpretation.

One major way to refresh our reading of familiar biblical stories is to shift our point of view, to consider the text through the eyes of biblical characters we may have neglected or that homiletical tradition has passed over. The way certain parables are named often reinforces a particular interpretation at the expense of another. We lose the nuances and complexities of a tale when it is labeled "The Good Samaritan." Is he the only character worth our attention? What about the robbers, the victim, the priests, the innkeeper? Or consider "The Prodigal Son." Is his behavior the sum and substance of the story? What about the older brother, the father, the citizen of the foreign country who hired the prodigal to feed pigs after he squandered his inheritance, the musicians at the banquet when he returns home?

Choose any story from the Bible and take the point of view of a character whose perspective is usually ignored by other preachers or by you. What do you see that you missed before? Write one page (double spaced, oral/aural style)[2] in which you retell the story from the point of view of the often-ignored character. In the pages that follow are some exercises that our students have written that may stimulate your own creative work.

Student Exercises

No one ever asks me how it felt to have a king demand your presence.
I suppose it's because women in my day are expected to look good and keep the house.
But we are not mere objects for the pleasure of men.
We are people. With feelings and thoughts of our own.

I remember feeling sad that night, thinking of my husband away at battle.
He was so dedicated, so determined to serve his God and his king.
That left me, home alone, thinking of him and praying for his return.
That's where my thoughts were that night, as I took my usual evening bath.
Little did I know I was being watched.
King David himself wanted my company.
I didn't know what to say. Or rather, I knew what I couldn't say. No.
A woman's rights in this world are more of an illusion than anything.
I won't deny that the King was handsome, charismatic, strong.
But I was a married woman, with a husband who loved and cherished me.
David loved and cherished my body from afar.
It was lust that drew him to me.
It was cowardice that made him kill my husband.
We don't talk about it. Ever.
I'm afraid of what might happen
if my real feelings escape.
It's not safe for a woman to make noise
even in the castle of the king. [3]

◇◇◇◇◇◇◇

In the book of Judges,
Jephthah's nameless daughter gets two lines.
In the first, she instructs her father
to make good on his vow to God
although the result will be her death.
In the second, she requests two months
to wander the mountains with her friends
before she dies.
I have always thought of this young woman
as unambiguously devout,
so willing to help her father keep his oath
that she surrenders her own life without protest.
I have been bewildered by her reaction,
unable to find myself in her selfless devotion.
But, it occurs to me now,
maybe Jephthah's daughter knew the story of the akedah.
Maybe when they were in the mountains
she and her friends told and retold the story of Isaac:
how his father led him to the mountain,
bound him, and placed him on the altar,
how the angel of God arrives just in time.
Maybe her two confident lines
belie her desperate hope
that Isaac's angel will intervene for her, too. [4]

◇◇◇◇◇◇◇

All those people praying "Blessed art thou among women" to me have no idea
what it was like to raise Jesus.
I don't mean raise Jesus from the dead; I mean RAISE Jesus.
There were many difficult moments:
For example, the time he stayed behind in the temple to teach when he was twelve,
and his father and I went crazy with worry.
The second hardest time was when he came home from his travels,
and I thought we'd have time to visit.
But then he stayed out all day and night with his friends, teaching and healing,
and when I tried to talk to him,
he had the nerve to ask, "Who is my mother?" Right in front of everybody.
And then he called his disciples his mother and his brothers.
But I was the one who stood at the foot of the cross.
When they crucified him.
The disciples hid in fear.
That was the hardest time.
I have been appropriated as the symbol of obedience, submission, and grace.
Let's leave those characterizations to my son.
I was just your average widowed mother,
hungering for a word with my son on his rare visit home.
I went home and cried that day.[5]

I thought I'd raised them better than this—
It always seemed like they had good sense.

Practical boys, good at fishing,
take after their father.

The trouble started
when they began hanging around with Simon.
They come home telling tall tales
about nets ripping with too many fish,
and two boats nearly sinking under the weight.
I'll believe that when I see it!

Then one day we're just out fishing,
and some guy they call Jesus
strolls along the shore,
and he calls over to Simon and Andrew,
who just get up and go with him.
And then he calls out to James and John!
Sure enough, they just get up and leave me there.
Now, who knows what will happen to them!
They're risking everything for this Jesus.

I thought I'd raised them better than this—
It always seemed like they had good sense. [6]

Notes

1. David Buttrick, *Homiletic: Moves and Structures* (Minneapolis: Fortress Press, 1987), 55.
2. See chapter 16 for instructions on writing in the oral/aural style.
3. Kyle Eugene Brooks.
4. Rachel Sommer.
5. Janine L. Schenone.
6. William F. Brown.

WHAT DO YOU SEE?

In the last chapter, we addressed our contemporary "perspectival consciousness" by considering a biblical story from a character who is usually neglected. Now we want to extend our perspectival consciousness beyond the biblical passage itself to the context in which we read the Bible, to where we are geographically and socially located.

In their book *Liberation Preaching*, Justo and Catherine González remind us that one way the preacher can gain new insight into a biblical text is to imagine it being studied and expounded in a different socio-political setting.[1] A classic example can be seen in the Bible studies recorded by Roman Catholic priest Ernesto Cardinal in *The Gospel in Solentiname*. Here a group of peasants living in a remote archipelago in Nicaragua in the 1970s under the oppressive Somosa regime gathered each Sunday to discuss the Gospel reading for the day. Their comments on the biblical texts open up whole new vistas for reading familiar texts afresh and illustrate the ways in which a change in social location can radically alter our interpretation of Scripture. This four-volume work has since become a classic in terms of its articulation of grassroots liberation theology.

We do not, however, have to travel across the globe to witness the ways in which sociocultural context can affect interpretation. Words that strike us one way when we are reading them in our study, for example, may take on an entirely new slant when we read them in a city park or a crowded train. Likewise, those same words may come across very differently to a person with a steady, adequate income than they do to a single working mother with sporadic employment and children to raise.

One of the additional benefits of undertaking the reading of Scripture in alternative locations is that doing so can place us more solidly in the midst of the everyday lives of the people to whom we are preaching and cause us to connect more deeply with the real worlds they inhabit. I (Nora) remember some years ago attending a lectionary-based Bible study my pastor husband was leading on the top floor of a downtown bank building at lunchtime. Parishioners from our suburban congregation came to the study in the midst of their busy work days, and what amazed me was how much more willing they were to talk back to biblical texts and to offer alternative perspectives on them when we met them on *their* everyday turf, rather than asking them to meet us on ours.

All too often, says Choan-Seng Song, preaching "makes no effort to wrestle with implications of indigenous wisdom and local ways of life for the Christian gospel. The result is obvious. Christianity has little impact outside the church."[2]

These various perspectives from different locations drive us to ask:

Preacher, what do you see? Not just as you read this book but as you live day by day. If it is not plumb lines and baskets of fruit and the images of an ancient, agrarian world, what do you see? What world emerges from your daily routines and the mass media that shape the public understanding of culture and politics? . . . *Preacher, what do you see?* [3]

Choose one passage of Scripture for a sermon and read it in your study or the library or whatever is the most common setting for you to begin your preparation. Then take the passage to a completely different setting: the train station, shopping mall, hospital, coffee shop. Look around at what you see. Read the passage in the different setting. Look around again. Read the passage again. Keep repeating the process. Then ask yourself and God: What is the word of God saying to the people who pass you, to the scenes you observe, to the economic and social structures that built and support the setting?

Draw on your experience to write a one-page (double-spaced, oral/aural style)[4] homiletical exercise on "The Word of God to _____" (fill in the setting where you read the text). In the pages that follow are some exercises that our students have written that may stimulate your own creative work.

Student Exercises

Reading the story of how Lazarus was raised from the dead
while sitting on the steps of the New Haven Free Public Library
during evening rush hour
was a challenging exercise.
When preparing sermons,
I intentionally try to avoid loud noise and distractions at all costs.
Reading this passage in the library setting
allowed me to actually witness
the pain that people and communities endure
as they wait, like Mary and Martha,
for Jesus to enter their lives.
Teenage single mothers, homeless citizens, inner city youth . . .
What if Jesus arrives too late?
What if Jesus never shows up?
The church is called to remind the world
that it is never too late
for God to redeem and enter our lives. [5]

◇◇◇◇◇◇◇

I sit in a coffee shop,
watching a Mondrian-style mobile move,
a half-empty chai tea and my laptop before me.
I drove here in a car,
after watching the evening news
with its list of daily disasters.
There is a homeless person selling flowers outside.

I tried not to make eye contact as I stepped inside.
I tried not to remember the commercial about feeding starving children.
That was easy though, because a commercial for designer clothes quickly followed it.
Around me I see a world filled with images and people
that I would very much like to ignore.
The culture ignores them,
and tells me that it would be fine for me to do so as well.
But Jesus tells me that each thing done or not done
for the least of these
is something done or not done for him. [6]

People walking
traffic
people talking, drinking coffee, laughing
street vendor on the corner, serving tacos
words on the screen, words on the page
trees making dappled shadows on the sidewalk
hawk perched on the cross.
The world is full of paradoxes:
nature's beauty on the one hand,
and people's busy-ness on the other hand,
all of it interspersed with the things we think we need.
Where's the space for stopping to sit for a spell like the hawk?
How to breathe calm life into this busy world,
to get it to stop and think for a minute?
How can I stop for long enough
to look at how Scripture interacts with my life,
And that of my parishioners? [7]

Notes

1. Justo L. González and Catherine Gunsalus González, *Liberation Preaching: The Pulpit and the Oppressed* (Nashville: Abingdon Press, 1980), 78–82.

2. Choan-Seng Song, "Preaching as Shaping Experience in a World of Conflict," in *Preaching as Shaping Experience in a World of Conflict*, ed. Prof. Dr. Albrecht Grözinger and Rev. Dr. Kang Ho Soon (Utrecht: Societas Homiletica, 2005), 22.

3. Thomas H. Troeger, *Imagining a Sermon* (Nashville: Abingdon Press, 1990), 16.

4. See chapter 16 for instructions on writing in the oral/aural style.

5. Tyrone Emmanuel McGowan Jr.

6. Joshua Alan Rodriguez.

7. Amy Spagna.

CREATING PARABLES FROM LIFE

John McClure writes, "Many parables take what listeners expect to hear and reverse it. For instance, in the New Testament story of the Pharisee and the publican, we assume that the original listener expected the Pharisee's prayer to be accepted by God and the publican's to be rejected. In the story, however, the opposite occurs, opening the listener to new meanings."[1]

"Reversals," Frank Thomas reminds us, "are fundamental to human life and human communication." They open us to new meanings and to a fresh encounter with God, which can become for our listeners an experience of unexpected grace. "*I have a sense of wonder about reversals,*" writes Thomas, "*because I suspect that the preacher's ability to offer an assurance of grace is grounded in the ability of the preacher to deal with reversals and paradox.*"[2]

It is instructive to note that most of Jesus' parables are not explicitly about religion even though they reveal essential insights into the nature of grace, forgiveness, and the reign of God. The story lines of the parables feature the commonest elements of life: building houses, finding a lost animal, rejoicing over the return of a child, sowing fields with an extravagant amount of seed, attending wedding receptions, baking bread, giving birth. Jesus fashions his stories out of the materials of life that were known to his listeners. The combination of reversed expectations and ordinary life settings made them highly listenable and memorable, qualities that we seek in sermons. Jesus' listeners might well have walked away from hearing him while they replayed the parable in their minds, mulling it over, reflecting on the surprise ending, and wondering about its implications for life and faith.

Create a parabolic story of not more than one page (double spaced, oral/aural style)[3] that draws on common experience and embodies the reversal of expectations. This might be a true story out of your life or entirely fictional or a blend of fact and fiction. The important thing is that it entices us to consider life or faith from a new and unexpected perspective. In the pages that follow are some exercises written by our students that may stimulate your own creative work.

Student Exercises

The kingdom of God is like playing poker with my grandma.
I know what you're thinking—
The kingdom of God simply cannot be like playing poker with your grandma.
First of all, Jesus said very little about grandmas and he never enjoyed a beer with a grandma

and he certainly never gambled with his grandma!
He would shake his head at politicians
who put a dress and some lipstick on a regressive tax and call it a "lottery" for schools.
He would have laughed at the cynicism
of those who would support the tribal rights of a beleaguered minority
in the hope of having a convenient casino just up the road, just out of sight.
He—I am sure—never once bluffed his way through a hand of Texas hold 'em.
But despite all that, I am absolutely convinced—
the kingdom of God is like playing poker with my grandma.
You see, when you play poker with my grandma, there's no money involved—just chips
And when you run out,
someone around the table (probably grandma) will slide another stack of chips your way
no questions asked, no tallies kept, because everyone knows the favor will be reversed soon enough.
When you play poker with my grandma
the iced tea is cold, and the snacks are ready at hand
and the only thing more noticeable than chips hitting the table
is the sound of laughter and storytelling that goes long into the night.
The kingdom of God truly is something like playing poker with my grandma.[4]

The kingdom of God may be compared to
a child's birthday party at Burger King in a small southern town.
The child, my child, was turning four years old.
The entire preschool class was invited to come. And come they did.
On the day of the party, we arrived at Burger King with fifteen four-year-old boys and girls.
They were black, like my Courtney, and white, like her best friend, Denise.
They were blond and red headed, Asian and Hispanic.
It was 1979 and we were an unusual sight.
An older white man sat across the restaurant . . . and watched.
We ate our lunch of hamburgers and fries . . . and the man kept watching.
The large circus cake appeared, candles ablaze, voices raised, Happy Birthday to You.
And the man watched still.
Courtney blew out the candles and all the children laughed and clapped.
Why was that man watching us? . . . What did he want? . . . Should I be worried?
Finally, presents received and favors distributed, the party was winding down.
A quick glance over my shoulder to see if he watched still . . . but he was gone.
Relieved, I opened my wallet to settle the bill.
"Oh, no, Ma'am," said the store manager. "Put your money away. The party is all paid for.
The man in the corner asked for the check and paid the bill."
The man who watched us . . .
"He said that watching you and the children had made his heart glow."
Sometimes the kingdom of God is an old white man in the corner booth at Burger King,
watching.[5]

Many people in Haiti have no shoes.
So on my last trip there I took a big duffel bag full of tennis shoes:
men's, women's, and children's.
I only gave the shoes to people who really needed them
and I made sure that they fit, because I was worried
they might try to sell them to someone else.
Jean Michel approached me: "May I have a pair of shoes?"
I looked at his and they were falling apart.
But I was down to my last pair, a men's eleven and a half.
"Let's see what size your shoes are." I knew they were much smaller.
He handed me his left shoe—it was a nine.
"I'm sorry," I said, "these new shoes are too big for you. You'll trip and fall."
"Please let me try them on," he said timidly.
"Maybe later, Jean Michel," I said. I was hoping he would drop it
or I would find someone else to give the shoes to.
But he didn't drop it. He kept pestering me the rest of the day.
(In a hopeful, almost desperate voice) "Let me just try the shoes on."
(Irritated) "Fine," I said, "But they aren't going to fit you.
These shoes are eleven and a half and you're wearing size nine."
Jean Michel howled with delight as his foot fit perfectly into the left shoe.
It took me a few moments to realize he had been wearing shoes
that were two and a half sizes too small.
That day I learned that even when I had the facts, I could still be wrong. [6]

I am not an athlete.
Each Friday in elementary school, I would stand shakily, swallowing my anxiety
as we stood in a group in the gym to pick teams.
Each week the other kids, the ones who could run fast, catch well, and throw straight
would be called one by one
peeling away from the group until only a few of us remained,
praying to ourselves, "Please don't let me be last this time."
One Friday, the gym teacher raised her bushy eyebrow at me and barked out my name to be captain.
A huge wave of relief came over me.
Now I could pick my team, and there was no way I could be picked last.
I selected the best athlete in the class, a paragon of strength and agility.
He lithely strode to line up behind me.
And then, in a clear and confident tone,
my opposing captain called out, "Kendra."
There was a long silence. Kendra stared at the captain, not moving.
I turned to the captain in disbelief.
Kendra was the girl who most frequently dropped the ball,
who most frequently kept me from being the last pick.
The girl who even now, as she walked stupefied to line up, tripped over her own feet.
Suddenly I felt my face grow hot as I was overcome by shame.

I looked at the captain, nine years old, standing calmly.
She turned to me and said, "Your pick."[7]

I'm pretty sure that the kingdom of God is like
the time a few falls ago
my great-grandma,
seeing that her neighbor's apple tree
had borne no fruit that year,
seeing her own apple tree,
groaning under the weight
of its own overabundance,
branches cracking,
sneaked out in the middle of the night
with a basket and some wire.
Slowly, through the night, she picked apples
from her own tree,
putting them in the basket until it was filled.
Then she went to the neighbor's apple tree,
and tied each apple from her own
onto the branches of the empty tree.
When her neighbor woke up the next morning,
she looked out her window to find
where there was scarcity, abundance,
and proceeded to make apple jelly and butter
for the rest of the block. [8]

Notes

1. John S. McClure, "Parabolic Communication," in *Preaching Words: 144 Key Terms in Homiletics* (Louisville, KY: Westminster John Knox Press, 2007), 99.

2. Frank A. Thomas, *They Like to Never Quit Praisin' God* (Cleveland, OH: The Pilgrim Press, 1997), 13. Emphasis is Thomas's.

3. See chapter 16 for instructions on writing in the oral/aural style.

4. Ryan C. Fleenor.

5. Marilyn Baugh Kendrix.

6. Sam Louis Owen.

7. Rebecca M. Floyd.

8. Jacob J. Erickson.

THE AMBIGUITIES OF TRADITION

Thomas Long observes that preachers go to Scripture with "prior understandings of the Christian faith embodied in rich theological traditions. A theological tradition is a complex, often ambiguous, but somewhat systematic way of seeing the Christian faith as a whole."[1] While we preach out of respect for the Christian traditions in which we stand, we also do so honestly acknowledging that traditions are "often ambiguous" because they have been used for evil as well as for good. As Teresa Fry Brown reminds us, "The Bible has been used to undergird the subjugation of women and various racial/ethnic groups and keep white Protestant males, who supposedly founded the United States on Christian principles, in positions of power. . . . African American Christians appropriated and reinterpreted biblical texts in order to live as free heirs of God's promise."[2]

The patterns of religious ambiguity reach back through centuries of church history. One way to read that past is to see it as a process of repeated appeals to the highest and holiest values of the tradition in order to correct its distortions. Orders of friars and nuns arose during the Middle Ages to challenge the corruption of the church hierarchy by reclaiming the values of community, service, and hospitality. Martin Luther returned to the Scriptures to find anew the centrality of grace in the life of faith when it had been buried by elaborate ecclesial practices. The Wesleys brought the heart-changing warmth of the gospel to people whom the church had ignored or marginalized. Martin Luther King Jr. carried on the tradition of the biblical prophets to stand against racial injustice when many churches remained silent about the evil and tragically reinforced it. Feminist and womanist theologians appealed to the scriptural affirmation that God made both male and female in the divine image and to the positive relationship between Jesus and women to confront the perversion of sexism. And this is only the briefest list. It does not begin to name all the local preachers who, century after century, drew upon the best of the tradition in order to make the church's practice more faithful to the gospel. It is an ongoing task because the church is never perfect but is in perpetual need of reform.

Write one page (double spaced, oral/aural style)[3] that draws upon the truth of faith in order to correct a distortion of faith. Draw upon the best of tradition in order to come to terms with the worst of tradition. In the pages that follow are some exercises written by our students that may stimulate your own creative work.

Student Exercises

"What's the opposite of faith?"
Father Gary put the question to me out of the blue, and I thought shamefully of my doubting times. Oh yes,
I knew the opposite of faith: insecurity, variability, a soul-sucking incapability to ever know.
"Certitude!" he said.
I blinked in surprise, wondering if I had heard wrong.
I thought of the years I had spent in Baptist Sunday School,
trying to work myself into faithful certitude,
trying to psych myself into a strong enough mental conviction,
so that I would feel brave enough to push that certitude into someone else's head,
and . . . drum role . . .
invite a friend to church—the best show of certitude a person could ever hope to offer.
But now—certitude as the opposite of faith?
What could this mean?
Father Gary began to speak of things I'd never heard before:
God the Mystery
the paradox of a divine Love made human.
Jesus, the invitation to live more naturally and love more genuinely than I ever had before.
I let the words wash over me,
washing away the desperation of recalcitrant certitude
and uncovering the real faith within that I'd never seen as such.[4]

I've spent a great part of my life's spiritual energy
trying to get over the pain of the particular theology I was taught as a child.
It all comes down to "atonement theory."
I've come to fear Easter—can I say that and still be called to the ministry?
Mostly I just avoid church during Holy Week.
I was taught that "God so loved"—
that love demanded that God kill his blameless, wonderful, perfect Son
because of me and my sins.
My sins—the little eight-year-old girl,
cowering in her bed at night and praying that she not die
because she was certain she was a "goat" and not a "sheep."
God as the ultimate child abuser—of God's only Son, and of me. How did this make sense?
Some part of me kept saying, "Not my God. That might make sense to you, but not to me."
I think we spend way too much time thinking about "Good" Friday and not enough about
    Easter. Resurrection, the Presence of Love, the Power of Love.
Crucifixion is what humankind did to Jesus, and continues to do to each other.
God did not/does not participate in that abuse.
Resurrection is where God is found.
In the midst of the death dealt of human violence, love breathes life back into brokenness.

I want to bring a message of hope and the power of Love
to people who have been guilt-ridden for too long.
I want to bring Joy back into the teaching of the church. [5]

Mmmm. Nothing like a just-picked apple.
Crisp to the teeth, at once sweet and tart, juice dancing across taste buds and down the throat.
Would you like a bite? Go on! It's delicious!
Oh—I see.
You heard that I brought about the fall of all humankind with the offer of just such a morsel.
That because of my disobedience, every human since has sweated or toiled for their fruit,
Or been twisted by the agonizing pangs of childbirth.
That because of my misguided nibble, women throughout history have been met with
Mistrust. Derision. Skepticism. Condescension.
Relegated to kitchens and nunneries and footnotes.
OK, so don't have a bite of this apple—but don't swallow that other story whole either.
Mine may have been the rebellion that plucked apple from the knowledge tree.
But there are so many other things at my very core—sweet, tart, refreshing, wonderful things.
I am mother to the loyalty of Ruth, as she made her home with Naomi.
To the brazenness of Rahab, hiding Joshua's spies under bundles of flax.
To the faith and courage of Mary who sang her "Yes" to God.
To the vision of Anna the prophetess, seeing the Christ even in a swaddled babe.
To the strength of women who have pushed boundaries and questioned stereotypes,
Who have led movements and spoken truth to power.
Who have dared to step into seminaries and pulpits,
to proclaim freedom to the captives and to one another.
I am no mere fruit peddler.
I am Eve, fruitful and multiplying. [6]

"I will give you the keys of the kingdom of heaven; whatever you bind on earth will be
    bound in heaven; and whatever you loose on earth will be loosed in heaven." Mt. 16:19
I wonder if Jesus really did say these words, and if he did, did he ever regret saying them?
Those keys have locked many out.
"You don't have the right credentials, beliefs, color, sex, sexuality, to represent 'the divine.'"
These keys have locked many in.
"But we have always done it this way. Look, it's in the book!"
Keys can make one feel falsely safe.
"I am on the right side." "I am on the left side." "I am on God's side."
People without the keys can feel alienated, subjugated, denigrated.
Non-key holders are often translated as being "less than human."
Pick any century—and think of what we have done in the name of those keys!
"You loose, you bind," becomes "You lose. You are bound."
Key, "a small instrument specifically cut to fit a lock and move its bolt"
seems too narrow a word to describe that which opens Your Kingdom,

I prefer other words—like blood, bits of broken bread, and love.
But key can mean something that affords access.
Is that what you meant to give us, Jesus, access?
I hope so, but I don't know.
What I do know is this—
At this moment in time, your sons and daughters are not ready to be given any keys.
Pray for us. [7]

Notes

1. Thomas G. Long, *The Witness of Preaching*, 2nd ed. (Louisville, KY: Westminster John Knox Press, 2005), 52.

2. Teresa L. Fry Brown, *God Don't Like Ugly: African American Women Handing on Spiritual Values* (Nashville: Abingdon Press, 2000), 114.

3. See chapter 16 for instructions on writing in oral/aural style.

4. Stephanie Wong.

5. Sandra L. Fischer.

6. Luanne Rose Panarotti.

7. Patricia Leonard Pasley.

REASON AND FEELING

In his book *Celebration and Experience in Preaching*, Henry Mitchell writes, "The hearer is to be involved holistically in the sermon event, in order to beget or nourish a faith that involves the entire person."[1] He later observes, "A rule of thumb for clarification of holistic purpose in sermon preparation is to ask, Am I struggling to get a point across or am I working at a flow in consciousness which will be used to beget trust and change behavior? Another way to put it is, Do I see and feel what I'm talking about, or am I myself obsessed with clever, scholarly data and abstract ideas?"[2]

Mitchell is not opposed to the use of reason in sermons. He writes extensively about why reason is essential, especially to provide clarity of thought. But he rightly eschews the illusion of believing that reason alone is adequate for conveying the Word of God. He sees that the heart has got to be as engaged as thoroughly as the intellect.

Choose one of the following words: faith, hope, love, justice. In no more than a sentence or two, define it in clear, analytical language. In other words, write your own theological "dictionary" definition of the term. Then use the rest of the page to help the term come alive in terms of human experience. You could do this through a story or an image or a personal testimony or a poem. The goal is to help the hearer "be involved holistically in the sermon event" by appealing both to reason and feeling, so that she or he can "see and feel" what you are preaching. In the pages that follow are some exercises written by our students that may stimulate your own creative work.

Student Exercises

To hope is to risk your heart
on that which has not yet made itself fully known.
Hope smells like beeswax melting
into the white, chipped-paint window sill of my childhood home.
As autumn days shortened
darkness falling earlier each day,
my mother would retrieve a set of brass candle sticks
and set them in the street-facing windows,
a protest against the darkness,
her way to say: there is a light that will not be overcome.

A protest against veils of deceit,
the violence of our street,
a way to say: this word is not the last,
and we will risk our hearts,
our little flames, to proclaim what is yet unknown:
the light of Christ that does not falter,
how ever long Earth's winter night may stretch into the year.
So my mother lit the honeyed wicks
to set the street aglow,
praying with each trembling flame,
come, Lord Jesus, come.[3]

◇◇◇◇◇◇◇◇

Hope: persistent opting for the future in the present of adversity.
There was no evidence that Dolores would ever own her own home.
In fact, all the evidence at hand pointed to the contrary.
She had late-stage cancer, the doctors said.
She could no longer care for her six-year-old son, the caseworker said.
She could no longer care for herself, the hospice team said.
I was part of the hospice team.
On the way to doctors' appointments, chemo sessions, the grocery store,
Dolores would sit in the passenger seat of my Chevy Silverado,
munch on corncobs and mashed potatoes from KFC,
and stare out the window as the suburban sprawl of Springfield passed by.
She'd talk about the cats she'd have on her estate,
elaborate cages for pet birds and rats and hamsters.
She'd describe her son's toy room,
with shelves and bins and hand-painted murals of his favorite TV characters.
She'd muse about her garden, a farm of sorts,
with peonies and chrysanthemums
and a tire swing hanging from an evergreen.
There was no evidence that Dolores would ever have any of these things;
in fact, all evidence pointed to the contrary.
But as we whizzed along I-91 in silence,
it was as if, despite the whirr of the engine and the whistle of the wind,
we were already feeding her cats,
playing with her son's toys,
swinging and digging and smelling the scent of pine.[4]

◇◇◇◇◇◇◇◇

Faith is the firm belief in something for which there is no proof,
and the least provable something in which people have faith . . . is God.
There is no proof of God in our world, but there is evidence everywhere.
I can feel God as each morning sunrise warms my skin.
I can hear God in the raucous laughter of a child, spinning in circles in the grass.

153

I can smell God as I walk among the hedgerows, densely entwined with honeysuckle.
I can taste God in the first bite of a crisp apple.
But mostly, God creeps into my being and fills my heart in music.
A shy child, I refused to go to Sunday school.
Regular school was difficult enough for me—having to talk to new people
and endure the noise of too many children in one small space.
So when Sunday came along I was not up for another day of being social.
No, I wouldn't stay in Sunday school, so my parents let me stay in church.
But they were both busy—Dad as an usher and Mom in the choir.
So they let me sit next to Jimmy, the organist.
I sat beside him on the organ bench during the service every Sunday.
I watched his feet play the foot pedals and I listened for God's voice in the bass notes.
I watched his hands skip from one keyboard to another with grace,
and the angels sang along.
He pushed and pulled the stops and I felt God's tone change, now flutes, now trumpets.
Jimmy and the organ pushed the breath of God through the pipes and music came out.
In that music, my faith in God was born.
I have no proof of God in this world,
But music is my best evidence.[5]

Faith: trust in the promises of God as God has revealed them to humankind.
Trusting even when everything seems hopeless.
Come with me, a US soldier, to Babylon—Central Iraq—in 2005.
You sit at the banks of the river Babylon, that famous river,
and everywhere you look you see devastation and ruin.
"How can I sing the Lord's Song in a foreign land?"
The military tanks and black hawks have destroyed
anything that was left of the Babylon which greeted the exiled Jews.
It is a dusty, brown, camouflage-covered mess.
You weep.
I wept. Because I felt helpless, hopeless, and faithless.
I didn't feel able to praise God.
I was too upset and too confused by what we had done to this country.
I took out my Bible and read through the Psalm.
I was feeling the rage and the anger of the Jews in Psalm 137.
And I began to see what faith really means.
The Jews expressed to God the rage they felt generated by their loss.
And through all of this, their faith remained.
The Psalm allowed me to be angry.
But it called me in my anger to trust in the promises of God
It showed me honest faith. Real faith.
Faith that accompanies you in your anger and your rage and transforms it to hope.
Sit with me by the bloody, muddy waters of Babylon,
and sing the Lord's song with me, because God is faithful.[6]

Justice is a burning desire to set the world aright,
To ensure that people get what they deserve,
What a person is owed for the very reason of being a person.
Justice is a feeling that grabs you in your gut.
It begins with anger
The day you take a single mother and her two children
To a wake for a cousin
Shot in the head on the street aged seventeen.
It begins with the sound
of a sixteen-year-old expressing grief,
inexpressible in words,
in a cry that becomes a scream
then sobbing.
It begins with a knowledge of helplessness
that what has been broken today
can never be mended
This sound, these tears, this grief, this family
will never truly be righted again.
It begins in grief, and rage, and helplessness.
Honest about its own idealism
its own impossible nature
justice moves to resolve:
never again.[7]

Hope is the active belief in something
without which a certain outcome would seem out of the realm of possibility.
My hand was not steady as I signed the book, I was nervous.
It was my first visit to this nursing home
And only yesterday was I transformed from being "me" to "hospice chaplain."
It was only a moment, but suddenly I just was. A title I was given, expected to be.
What am I doing? Who am I kidding? Everyone here can see I don't have a clue.
I walked down the long corridor, referring to my chart every ten steps. Room 112. 112.
Before I entered the room I heard a single male voice, talking. Gentle. Almost melodious.
That is strange, I thought. I know she has been unresponsive for years.
I timidly entered the room, trying to look together, competent.
I saw them together.
She was as I expected—eyes open, staring blankly at the ceiling,
shirt soaked from the constant stream of drool.
And there he was, holding her hand. Gently talking, wiping her mouth, stroking her cheek.
They had been married as teenagers. "She was my high school sweetheart," he tells me.
He comes every day. Only missed one day in seven years because of a snowstorm.
She has not recognized him for five years. He sits. Reads to her. Tells her stories. Holds her.

Reminds the nurses to put in her hearing aids. "She can't hear without them," he tells me.
I can feel his love for her from where I am sitting.
I see him brush the hair away from her face and gaze into her empty blue eyes.
"I love you, Dottie. My Dottie."
Leaving a tender kiss on her cheek and a whisper of hope in her ear.[8]

Notes

1. Henry H. Mitchell, *Celebration and Experience in Preaching* (Nashville: Abingdon Press, 1990), 18.
2. Ibid., 55.
3. Mary Emily Briehl Duba.
4. Matthew D. Cortese.
5. Marilyn Baugh Kendrix.
6. Catriona Laing.
7. Matthew McClelland Lukens.
8. Bethany Leigh Myers.

CELEBRATION IN PREACHING

Henry Mitchell says that one of the hallmarks of African-American preaching is that frequently its sermons build to a climax of pure celebration and thanksgiving to God. He writes, "Whatever the style used, be it narrative, rhetoric, or whatever, the celebration expresses gladness about what God has done and is doing in the same area in which it is the purpose to engender growth. In other words, the affirmation celebrated must be the very same affirmation as that taught and experienced in the main body of the sermon."[1]

James Earl Massey draws a strong link between the celebration exhibited in black preaching and the pain and struggle out of which it is born:

> Whatever festivity and playfulness fill the black sermon are there because they have been *won* in the midst of sorrow and lament, making the sermon itself an open expression of faith that has worked its way through, and now speaks in praise of God. This amounts, really to a depth theology of soul-worship. The festivity which results in this way is never an opiate there, and the playfulness is not calculated escapism. The black sermon celebrates remembered victories in the midst of raw demands.[2]

In his book *They Never Like to Quit Praisin' God*, Frank Thomas reminds us that such preaching not only lifts the spirits of its hearers; it also encourages and empowers them: "The sermonic design is an emotional process that culminates in a moment of celebration when the good news (the assurance of grace) intensifies in core belief until one has received an inner assurance, affirmation, courage, and a feeling of empowerment. One experiences oneself as victorious (i.e., saved, set free, healed, encouraged, etc.) regardless of the external tragic circumstances of life."[3]

Although Mitchell, Massey, and Thomas are all writing out of the African-American preaching tradition, their insights are important for preachers of every tradition. When we say "We preach the gospel," we are saying "We preach good news." Good news?! When is the last time you heard or read good news as the lead story on the radio or television or website? News by its very nature tends to be about the bad things that are happening. Crises, crashes, and catastrophes grab the headlines. The Bible itself portrays without reserve the sadness and heartbreak of human life, and gives expression to poignant lament. But the Bible also affirms that at the deep, dear core of things there is a grace, a love, a compassion that is everlasting and irrepressible, and that is indeed good news—a joy that no heart that has tasted it can restrain.

Write one page (double spaced, oral/aural style)[4] that does nothing but celebrate something that God has done or is doing either in the Bible or in life here and now. Your goal is to communicate the heart-dancing, soul-singing, mind-lifting joy of God's action. To get into the spirit of this exercise, you might read Psalm 148 and Psalm 150. In the pages that follow are some exercises written by our students that may stimulate your own creative work.

Student Exercises

Amazing Grace!
Can you hear what I'm saying?
I'm talking about old, dried-up wells gushing
life water, oceans deep.
I'm talking about valleys of brittle bones rising.
I'm talking about thick honey oozing from rocks.
I'm talking about Amazing Grace.
These blind eyes have seen God's salvation
a light of revelation to the nations.
Can you see it?
The weak are strong! The oppressed are free!
The givers receive! The broken are whole!
The lost are found! The lonely are befriended!
The humble are exalted! The mourners are comforted!
Our weary hearts have a place for rest.
Wondrous. Abundant. Sufficient.
Amazing.
Undeserved, Unwarranted, Unmerited
Grace.
Amazing Grace.
Can you hear what I'm saying?[5]

God, we thank you for the many gifts of your creation.
For the sun that warms us,
the stars that guide us through the night,
and the crescent moon that calls upon the nightingale to sing;
God, for these gifts, we thank you.
For waters that bathe us, air that sustains us,
and earth of red clay that moves the hands of the potter at her wheel;
God, for these gifts, we thank you.
For mountains and mist that inspire poems written in Chinese calligraphy,
for the drips and drops of scattered rainfall that inspire rhythms beaten on African drums,
for spring grass that invites children to dance barefoot,
for fire, for elephants, for fragrant lavender,
for multicolored pigeons that remind us that even the humble can fly,
and for the tiniest dandelion seeds, flying in the breeze,
carrying our dreams to places beyond our imagination;
God, for these gifts, we thank you.

We face the world in awe.
God, help our creations, inspired by yours, be true to your vision.
Let our celebration inspire our sisters and brothers
to rediscover your love, alive in this world, today and every day.[6]

When I reflect on the active presence of God in my life,
all I can do is join in and sing
the life giving lyrics
of that great hymn of the church,
Great is Thy Faithfulness.
Even when I am unfaithful
God still remains faithful.
Morning by morning new mercies I see.
I can truly say that
everything I have needed God has provided.
Since my arrival in New Haven
I have continually stood in awe
at how God has made ways for me
when there was no way.
In spite of the challenges that have come my way,
I can still see how God has ordered and directed
my steps along this journey.
I am filled with joy because
I know that God is not finished working.
Because of all the Lord's benefits and blessings
I will continue to bless the Lord
with every fiber of my being.
For the Lord is worthy to be praised!
I will gladly offer God total praise.[7]

Oh Divine Breath,
You, whose wind never ceases,
You wrap around me like a cloak on a cold day.

Your breath collapses time.
You breathe through me,
As You have breathed through the generations before me.
I am connected to them through You.
Your breath was there when You parted the waters,
Leading my people to freedom as You exhaled.
And You were there when they reached the promised land
As You breathed through their songs of praise.

Your breath collapses the distance we create in our world.
My exhale becomes the breath breathed into those who I will never meet, countries away.
And my inhale receives the carried breath of the downtrodden and the privileged alike.
In You, we are united.

Oh Divine Breath,
You rejuvenate my soul, and You still my angst.
How great is Your unceasing wind![8]

◇◇◇◇◇◇◇◇

"Mary Magdalene went and announced to the disciples: 'I have seen the Lord.'" (John 20:18)
One Easter, ten years after the fall of apartheid,
I was in a rickety church in a South African township
for a gathering of the black churchwomen's guild,
the Women's Manyano.
"I know that Christ is risen!" cried an elderly woman,
"Because I and my children can go anywhere in this city,
ride on any bus and cast my vote for whoever I want."
Creak, creak went the wooden pews as
the mass of our bodies heaved as we joined in the cheer.
"I know that Christ is risen!" sang the pastor,
"Because he sent women first to tell the world,
and now women like us can be pastors
and say that we have seen the Lord!"
Thump, thump, went the hand on the leather cushion,
Marking the beat for the song of our hearts.
"I know that Christ is risen!" called a woman nursing a child,
"Because today we can worship with our white sisters and coloured sisters
and tell the world that we have seen the Lord!"
Sing, sing, went the voice of our hearts,
as the hymn broke out and rose into the air,
and a hundred women danced because they had seen the Lord.[9]

Notes

1. Henry H. Mitchell, *Celebration and Experience in Preaching* (Nashville: Abingdon Press, 1990), 18.
2. James Earl Massey, *The Burdensome Joy of Preaching* (Abingdon Press, 1998), 102.
3. Frank A. Thomas, *They Never Like to Quit Praisin' God: The Role of Celebration in Preaching* (Cleveland, OH: Pilgrim Press, 1997), 31.
4. See Chapter 16 for instructions on writing in the oral/aural style.
5. Joshua Ashton Hill.
6. Chad Tanaka Pack.
7. Tyrone Emmanuel McGowan Jr.
8. Elizabeth Bonney.
9. Ellen Liesel Wakeham.

THE HUNGRY HEART

William Sloane Coffin, the Yale University activist chaplain who later became senior pastor of The Riverside Church in New York City, once said that if we preach deeply enough to ourselves—to our own hungers and longings and fears—we will also touch a common chord with the rest of humanity. Such preaching is not *about* ourselves, but *to* ourselves. In fact, such sermons may not include a single reference to our own life story and experience.

To understand this concept, call to mind, if you can, a sermon that you may have heard from another preacher that totally engaged you. The preacher did not once say your name or mention a single thing about you in the sermon, and yet you felt as though the whole sermon were addressed directly to you. It touched you at the deepest level of your being, engaging the questions, the perplexities, the hopes and fears that hold your attention and shape your visions and actions. It is highly possible that the sermon you are remembering was a sermon preached to the preacher's own deep self, and it connected to your humanity so strongly because it was also deeply connected to the preacher's humanity.

Gardner Taylor has observed that preaching to oneself brings with it a beneficial acknowledgement of the preacher's need for humility:

> The magnificent anomaly of preaching is to be found in the fact that the person who preaches is in need himself or herself of the message which the preacher believes he or she is ordained to utter. How dare such a person address others, in the name of God, who are no worse off than the spokesman! This is an almost incredible presumptuousness which ought to prompt every preacher to pray with anguish and bewilderment in the spirit of the words of the song of my own forebears, "It ain't my brother and it ain't my sister, but it's me, O Lord, standing in the need of prayer."[1]

In one page (double spaced, oral/aural style)[2] preach a sermon *to* yourself, not about yourself. Let it be a word you hunger to hear in the depths of your soul. In the pages that follow are some exercises written by our students that may stimulate your own creative work.

Student Exercises

Dear Self,
Have you ever counted how many people in the Bible have massive to-do lists
or brag about their impossibly tight schedules?

Not many.
Have you ever noticed how many are praised for running themselves ragged?
Not many.
What about biblical heroes who heed the call to rest and be still?
They're all over the book.
Holy Rest. It is not an oxymoron.
It is a commandment.
It is not a special treat you grant yourself if you've been good;
or a reward only for the days when everything else has been done.
It is a posture of praise,
a practice of humility,
a reminder that the world does not start with and end with and depend upon you.
You acknowledge that others deserve your full-spirited and healthy presence,
and remind them that they, too, deserve and require rest.
Dear Self,
you are beloved when you move and when you are still.
Have faith, and be still.[3]

I want to hear a word from God
in an uncertain world,
I want to hear a plan
what I should do with my life
or, at least, my week,
my afternoon.

I don't want to hear watered-down,
easy-to-follow instructions,
whispered from a timid church,
desperate not to scare me away.
I want to hear something real.
Something hard.
Something Christian.

I want to hear about reckless hope
when human suffering breaks your heart.
About stubborn courage
when fear makes more sense.
About choosing sacrifice
and suffering when life could be easy.

I want to hear a word from God.
But I'm not sure I want to listen.[4]

You are loved.
Yes, you.
Not because you prayed this morning when you normally forget.
And not because you smiled at someone who looked sad.
You are loved in a way that even you,
working on your fancy Master's degree and using all those big words like
existential, hermeneutical, post-structuralist, deconstructionist—
half of which you don't quite know how to use properly, by the way—
yes, even you can't understand.
You are loved because you are just as you are.
Broken, sad, and alone.
Rejected, lost, and carrying the weight of your history on your shoulders—
from the moment you get up to the moment you settle into sleep—
you are loved.
You might not even believe it. In fact you don't.
But there it is.
Remember that there is nothing that you can do to take that away.
No matter how many words you butcher in the course of your studies,
no matter who you don't smile at or how many times you forget to pray.
It is the kind of irrational, unreasonable, nonsense kind of love
that pushes the planets in their course, builds mountains,
breaks the bonds of oppression
and offers itself to your imagination.
You are loved.[5]

◇◇◇◇◇◇◇◇

Your son did not die in vain.
No life is wasted,
not even one wracked with depression and despair.
His pain is gone
and though your heart is broken,
I am with you, just as I was with him.
You believe that he felt completely alone at the end,
but I was with him.
He may not have felt my presence,
but I was there.
Trust in this:
He did not die alone.
and I will help you make something good of this.
There is so much pain and brokenness in this world
and those who have experienced that pain
are truly my hands and feet,
my ability to minister to all of my children.
I need for you to use your grief to help others.
I have work for you to do to turn your mourning into dancing.

I can't bring him back to you in this life
but you will be reunited with him in joy.
"All of us go down to the dust;
Yet even at the grave we make our song:
Alleluia, alleluia, alleluia." (Book of Common Prayer, *499).*[6]

Notes

1. Gardner C. Taylor, *How Shall They Preach* (Elgin, IL: Progressive Baptist Publishing House, 1977), 27.
2. See chapter 16 for instructions on writing in the oral/aural style.
3. Kara June Scroggins.
4. William F. Brown.
5. Laura C. Smith.
6. Elaine Ellis Thomas.

THE PURPOSES
OF PREACHING

It is possible to polish the methods of creating and delivering sermons and yet lose sight of the purposes of preaching. You go through the motions, but without any clear goal the task becomes mechanical. R. W. Dale once observed, "We shall preach to no purpose unless we have a purpose in preaching." He goes on to quote Archbishop Whately, who said of a preacher, "he aimed at nothing, and hit it."[1]

What, then, are you aiming for when you preach? Are you aiming for the transformation of people? Then you might resonate with Teresa Fry Brown's affirmation that "the purpose of preaching is to present the acknowledged word of God, regardless of translation, verbally and nonverbally with such presence, power, passion and purpose that the listener or observer senses the impulse of change or conversion in his or her own life. Through sacred conversation channeled from God through the preacher with the people, transformation is effected."[2] Are you aiming to nurture a deep theological and biblical understanding of life? Then you may be drawn to E. K. Nhiwatiwa's statement: "If the preachers are not fully grounded in theology and biblical interpretation, what the members absorb will be superficial."[3]

Or are you aiming to build a relationship between the listeners and the empowering presence of God? If so you may resonate with this declaration by Christine Smith: "I preach because I believe in the grace-filled presence and power of a liberating God. God's presence is sheer gift—and constantly with us—enabling our own work of creation, redemption, and liberation."[4]

Clearly there is no single, simple answer to the question "Why do I preach?" and over the years the purposes of your preaching may change as you find yourself in new situations or as you undergo life-transforming experiences that refocus your faith and theological understanding of the gospel. But the question "Why do I preach?" can draw you anew to the well of living water, to the rush of sacred wind, and the warmth of the Spirit's fire.

Write a one-page sermon (double spaced, oral/aural style)[5] you would like to preach to a congregation of preachers on the purpose(s) of preaching. Speak from your heart, and let what you say reflect your deepest beliefs about what preaching should aim to be and do. In the pages that follow are some exercises written by our students that may stimulate your own creative work.

Student Exercises

My friends, if I can only share one piece of advice,
let it be this: tell the truth.
Seems simple enough, until you start putting it into practice.
You realize that parts of the scripture
don't sit as well as your sensibilities would like them to.
You discover that speaking prophetically
tends to go against the comfortable grain.
Perhaps you discover that your homiletical ability
suffers through creative doldrums or a heavy heart.
II Timothy offers us a charge we must not forget:
"Proclaim the message; be persistent
whether the time is favorable or unfavorable;
convince, rebuke, and encourage, with the utmost patience in teaching."
My friends, this is the work of telling the TRUTH,
of sharing the unadulterated gospel of Jesus Christ.
It is hard work that tears at your seams
and troubles your soul,
if you stick with it long enough.
The work of preaching is a life sentence
constraining you to the hard labor of communicating
in and through God's love.
It is the key to unchained joy and abundant living.
Tell the truth: it shall make all of us free.[6]

◇◇◇◇◇◇◇◇

Jesus was a trouble-maker.
That's what the Gospels tell us in their own distinct ways.
Turning over tables in the temple,
calling himself the Messiah,
teaching about the first being last—
Trouble with a capital T.
Jesus wasn't out to make friends.
He was out to bring the kingdom of God to fruition here on earth.
And that kingdom did not—
and does not—
look like the status quo.
It was and is trouble.
As the church we are called to continue in the great legacy Jesus began,
a legacy of trouble and turning over tables
and speaking out against the way it always has been.
We will be opposed.
We will be called trouble-makers.

This is a sign we're doing something right.
Do not be discouraged
when the world pushes back against the kingdom come.
Do not be discouraged,
but instead,
rejoice in our duty of divine trouble making![7]

There's a song in the musical "Little Shop of Horrors"
Sung by Audrey II, the giant Venus-fly-trap-space-plant
Called "Feed Me!"
That's what I would say to a congregation of preachers
That's what I say every time I sit down in the pews
Feed Me!
You can vary my diet
Make it prophetic or sad
Or funny or charming
Full of historical facts, Greek verbs, or stories about your cat
Just
Serve me up the Word of God!
I'm hungry
I'm just about starved
For some Good News
So please, please, please
Don't give me junk
Or empty calories.
Feed Me!
Don't preach something to me
You wouldn't want to hear yourself
Don't serve me something
You wouldn't want to eat.[8]

I carried a lot of baggage in here this morning.
My left shoulder aches from the weight of a recent salary cut.
My right one burns from the burden of my mortgage.
In my mouth I carry the bitter taste of a parent-teacher conference.
On my sleeve I wear the grief of a broken relationship.
In my heart I cradle the hurt of a broken world.
And my head is swimming in search for meaning.
Curtis Mayfield said I don't need no baggage, just get on board.
But the train's a-coming and I'm just too weighed down to jump on.
Relieve me.
Relieve me with stories of the mercy of God.
Relieve me with tales of the love of Jesus Christ.

167

Relieve me with that old familiar story,
that good news.
But whatever you do,
don't let me leave my baggage on the platform.
All that hurts and burns and grieves and searches,
that's mine too.
Just give me a hand
so I can thank the Lord.[9]

◇◇◇◇◇◇◇

Preacher, what do you fear?
The prophets walk before you,
straightening your paths, clearing the way.
The Apostles teach and lead you,
sharing the gift of the promised Spirit of truth
and binding you in love to those who came before,
and those who will come after.
That Spirit broods over you now,
calling forth from the formless waters of your mind
a new creation, fresh words for telling the eternal story:
God has done great things for us.
You share the everlasting company
of the Saints and Angels in glory,
adding your words of praise
to their great crescendo before the throne.
You know the honor and the pain of Mary,
who bore the eternal Word:
that Word is born again each day in you.
Preacher, fear not.
For you bear glad tidings of great joy,
hope for a fearful world.[10]

Notes

1. R. W. Dale, *Nine Lectures on Preaching: The 1876 Yale Lectures* (Doran, 1900), 24, as cited in John R. W. Stott, *Between Two Worlds: The Art of Preaching in the Twentieth Century* (Grand Rapids, MI: Wm. B. Eerdmans Publishing Company, 1982), 249.

2. Teresa L. Fry Brown, "The Action Potential of Preaching," in *Purposes of Preaching*, ed. Jana Childers (St. Louis, MO: Chalice Press, 2004), 50.

3. E. K. Nhiwatiwa, in *Preaching as God's Mission*, ed. Tsuneaki Kato (Tokyo: Kyo Bun Kwan, 1999), 157.

4. Christine Smith, "Preaching: Hospitality, De-Centering, Re-membering, and Right Relations," in *Purposes of Preaching*, 92.

5. See chapter 16 for instructions on writing in the oral/aural style.

6. Kyle Eugene Brooks.

7. Abigail M. Ferjak.

8. Kathryn L. Reinhard.

9. Jonah Smith-Bartlett.

10. Dane E. Boston.

Above the Moon Earth Rises: Hymn texts, anthems, and poems for a new creation, by Thomas H. Troeger (Oxford: Oxford University Press, 2002).

The Audacity of Preaching: The Lyman Beecher Lectures Yale Divinity School 1961, by Gene Bartlett (New York: Harper, 1962).

Best Advice for Preaching, edited by John S. McClure (Minneapolis: Fortress Press, 1998).

Between Two Worlds: The Art of Preaching in the Twentieth Century, by John R. W. Stott (Grand Rapids: Wm. B. Eerdmans Publishing Company, 1982).

Birthing the Sermon: Women Preachers on the Creative Process, edited by Jana Childers (St. Louis: Christian Board of Publication, 2001).

The Book of Legends/Sefer ha-Aggada: Legends from Talmud and Midrash, by Chajim Nachman Bialik and Yehoschua Hana Ravnitzky (New York: Schocken, 1992).

Borrowed Light: Hymn texts, prayers and poems, by Thomas H. Troeger (Oxford: Oxford University Press, 1994).

The Burdensome Joy of Preaching, by James Earl Massey (Nashville: Abingdon Press, 1998).

Celebration and Experience in Preaching, by Henry H. Mitchell (Nashville: Abingdon Press, 1990).

The Certain Sound of the Trumpet: Crafting a Sermon of Authority, by Samuel D. Proctor (King of Prussia, PA: Judson Press, 1994).

A Chorus of Witnesses: Model Sermons for Today's Preacher, by Thomas G. Long (Grand Rapids: Wm. B. Eerdmans Publishing, 1994).

Creating Fresh Images for Preaching: New Rungs for Jacob's Ladder, by Thomas H. Troeger (King of Prussia, PA: Judson Press, 1982).

The Divine Voice: Christian Proclamation and the Theology of Sound, by Stephen H. Webb (Grand Rapids: Brazos Press, 2004).

Envisioning the Word: The Use of Visual Images in Preaching, with CD-ROM, by Richard A. Jensen (Minneapolis: Fortress Press 2005)

The Essential Herbert, edited by Anthony Hecht (New York: Ecco Press, 1987).

Feasting on the Word, Year B, 6th Sunday in Lent (Minneapolis: Westminster John Knox Press, 2008).

Frames of Mind: The Theory of Multiple Intelligences, by Howard Gardner (New York: Basic Books, 1993).

Getting the Word Across: Speech Communication for Pastors and Lay Leaders, by G. Robert Jacks (Grand Rapids: Wm. B. Eerdmans Publishing Co., 1995).

God Don't Like Ugly: African American Women Handing on Spiritual Values, by Teresa L. Fry Brown (Nashville: Abingdon Press, 2000).

Graceful Speech: An Invitation to Preaching, by Lucy Lind Hogan (Louisville: Westminster John Knox Press, 2006).

HarperCollins Bible Commentary (San Francisco: HarperCollins San Francisco, 1988).

The HarperCollins Study Bible, New Revised Standard Version, edited by Wayne A. Meeks (New York: HarperCollins Publishers, 1993).

Harper's Bible Dictionary, edited by Paul J. Achtemeier with the Society of Biblical Literature (New York: HarperCollins Publishers, 1985).

A Healing Homiletic: Preaching and Disability by Kathy Black (Nashville: Abingdon Press, 1996).

A History of Preaching, by O. C. Edwards, Jr. (Nashville: Abingdon Press, 2004).

Homiletic: Moves and Structures, by David Buttrick (Minneapolis: Fortress Press, 1987).

The Homiletical Plot: The Sermon as Narrative Art Form, expanded edition, by Eugene Lowry (Louisville: Westminster John Knox Press, 2001).

How Shall They Preach, by Gardner C. Taylor (Elgin, IL: Progressive Publishing House, 1977).

The Hum: Call and Response in African American Preaching, by Evans Crawford (Nashville: Abingdon Press, 1995).

I Believe, I'll Testify: The Art of African American Preaching, by Cleophus J. LaRue (Louisville: Westminster John Knox Press, 2011).

The "I" of the Sermon, by Richard L. Thulin (Eugene, OR: Wipf and Stock Publishers, 2004).

"Imagination and Meticulousness, Haggadah and Halakhah in Judaism and Christian Preaching," by Alexander Deeg, in *Homiletic* 34:1 (2009), 1-11. (www.homiletic.net/index,php/homiletic/article/view/3315/1544)

Imagination of the Heart: New Understandings in Preaching, by Paul Scott Wilson (Nashville: Abingdon Press, 1988).

Imagining a Sermon, by Thomas H. Troeger (Nashville: Abingdon Press, 1990).

Imagining God: Theology and the Religious Imagination, by Garrett Green (Grand Rapids: Wm. B. Eerdmans Publishing Company, 1988).

Intelligence Reframed, by Howard Gardner (New York: Basic Books, 1999).

John Calvin, On the Christian Faith, edited by John T. McNeill (Liberal Arts Press, Inc., 1957).

Joy Songs, Trumpet Blasts, and Hallelujah Shouts! Sermons in the African-American Preaching Tradition, by Carlyle Fielding Stewart, III (Lima, OH: CSS Publishing, 1997).

Kindling Desire for God: Preaching as Spiritual Direction, by Kay L. Northcutt (Minneapolis: Fortress Press, 2009).

Liberation Preaching: The Pulpit and the Oppressed, by Justo L. and Catherine G. González, edited by William D. Thompson (Nashville: Abingdon Press, 1980).

Manual on Preaching, by Milton Crum Jr. (King of Prussia, PA: Judson Press, 1977).

Multiple Intelligences in the Classroom, by Thomas Armstrong (Alexandria, VA: Association for Supervision and Curriculum Development, 2000).

Nine Lectures on Preaching: The 1876 Yale Lectures, by R. W. Dale (Toronto: Doran, 1900).

North German Church Music in the Age of Buxtehude, by Geoffrey Webber (Oxford: Oxford University Press, 1996).

On Christian Doctrine, by St. Augustine; translated by D. W. Robertson Jr. (Indianapolis: Bobbs-Merrill Educational Publishing, 1958).

The Oxford Classical Dictionary, third edition, edited by Simon Hornblower and Antony Spawforth (Oxford: Oxford University Press, 1996).

Partners in Preaching: Clergy & Laity in Dialogue, Reuel L. Howe (New York: The Seabury Press, 1967).

Patterns for Preaching: A Sermon Sampler, edited by Ronald J. Allen (St. Louis: Chalice Press, 1998).

Performing the Word: Preaching as Theatre, by Jana Childers (Nashville: Abingdon, 1998).

Philippians: Interpretation: A Commentary for Teaching and Preaching, by Fred B. Craddock (Louisville: Westminster John Knox Press, 1984).

Picture Palace, by Paul Theroux (Boston: Houghton Mifflin Company, 1978).

Power in the Pulpit: How America's Most Effective Black Preachers Prepare Their Sermons, edited by Cleophus J. LaRue (Louisville: Westminster John Knox Press, 2002).

Practicing the Presence of God: A Homiletic from an Asian American Perspective, by Eunjoo Mary Kim (King of Prussia, PA: Judson Press: 1999).

"The Preacher, Text, and People," by Walter Brueggemann, in Theology Today 47 (October 1990).

Preaching, by Fred B. Craddock (Nashville: Abingdon Press, 1985).

Preaching as God's Mission, edited by Kato Tsuneaki (Tokyo: Kyo Bun Kwan, 1999).

Preaching as Local Theology and Folk Art, by Leonora Tubbs Tisdale (Minneapolis: Fortress Press, 1997).

Preaching as Shaping Experience in a World of Conflict, edited by Albrecht Grözinger and Kang Ho Soon (Societas Homiletica, 2005)

Preaching as Testimony, by Anna Carter Florence (Louisville: Westminster John Knox Press, 2007).

Preaching Justice: Ethnic and Cultural Perspectives, edited by Christine Marie Smith (Cleveland: United Church Press, 1998).

The Preaching Life, by Barbara Brown Taylor (Boston: Cowley Publications, 1993).

Preaching Mark in Two Voices, by Brian K. Blount and Gary V. Charles (Louisville: Westminster John Knox Press, 2002).

Preaching the Story, by Edmund A. Steimle, Morris J. Niedenthal, Charles Rice (Minneapolis: Fortress Press, 1980).

Preaching With Sacred Fire: An Anthology of African American Sermons, 1750 to the Present, edited by Martha Simmons and Frank A. Thomas (New York: W. W. Norton & Co., 2010).

Preaching Words: 144 Key Terms in Homiletics, by John S. McClure (Louisville: Westminster John Knox Press, 2007).

Prophetic Preaching: A Pastoral Approach, by Leonora Tubbs Tisdale (Louisville: Westminster John Knox Press, 2011).

Purposes of Preaching, edited by Jana Childers (St. Louis: Chalice Press, 2004).

The Recovery of Preaching, by Henry Mitchell (San Francisco: Harper & Row, 1977).

"Breaking Through the Screen of Cliché," by Nora Gallagher in *Reflections: Yale Divinity School* (Vol. 96, No. 2, Fall 2009).

The Riverside Preachers, edited by Paul H. Sherry (Cleveland: Pilgrim Press, 1978).

The Roundtable Pulpit: Where Leadership and Preaching Meet, by John S. McClure (Nashville: Abingdon Press, 1995).

Saved from Silence: Finding Women's Voice in Preaching by Mary Lin Hudson and Mary Donovan Turner (Chalice Press, 1999).

Sharing the Word: Preaching in the Round Table Church by Lucy Atkinson Rose (Louisville: Westminster John Knox Press, 1997).

Sing with Understanding: An Introduction to Christian Hymnology, second edition, revised and expanded, by Harry Eskew and Hugh T. McElrath (Nashville: Church Street Press, 1995).

So That All Might Know: Preaching That Engages the Whole Congregation, by Thomas H. Troeger and H. Edward Everding Jr. (Nashville: Abingdon Press, 2008).

Speaking from the Heart: Preaching with Passion, by Richard Ward (Nashville: Abingdon Press, 1992).

Speaking of the Holy: The Art of Communication in Preaching, by Richard F. Ward (St. Louis: Chalice Press, 2001).

The Spiritual Wisdom of the Gospels for Christian Preachers and Teachers, by John Shea (Liturgical Press).

Strength to Love, by Martin Luther King Jr. (Minneapolis: Fortress Press, 1981).

Telling the Truth: Preaching about Sexual and Domestic Violence, edited by John S. McClure and Nancy J. Ramsay (Cleveland: United Church Press, 1998).

They Never Like to Quit Praisin' God: The Role of Celebration in Preaching, by Frank A. Thomas (Cleveland: Pilgrim Press, 1997).

Transforming Bible Study: A Leader's Guide by Walter Wink (Nashville: Abingdon Press, 1989).

Transforming the Stone: Preaching Through Resistance to Change, by Barbara K. Lundblad (Nashville: Abingdon, 2001).

The United Methodist Hymnal (Nashville: The United Methodist Publishing House, 1989).

The Uses of Scripture in Recent Theology, by David H. Kelsey (Minneapolis: Fortress Press, 1975).

When the People Say No: Conflict and the Call to Ministry, by James Dittes (San Francisco: Harper & Row, 1979).

The Witness of Preaching, second edition, by Thomas G. Long (Louisville: Westminster John Knox Press, 2005).

The Women's Bible Commentary, edited Carol A. Newsom and Sharon H. Ringe (Louisville: Westminster/John Knox Press, 1992).

Made in the USA
Lexington, KY
28 December 2018